40 GREAT RAIL-TRAILS
in Michigan, Illinois and Indiana

Roger Storm

Susan Wedzel

Karen-Lee Ryan

Mike Ulm

♦♦♦

RAILS-TO-TRAILS CONSERVANCY
SATURN CORPORATION

Cover and interior design: Cutting Edge Graphics

All photographs by Roger Storm, Susan Wedzel, Karen-Lee Ryan or Mike Ulm, unless otherwise credited

Maps by Greg Blanchard, Rails-to-Trails Conservancy

✹ Printed on recycled paper

ISBN 0-925794-08-2

Manufactured in the United States of America

10 9 8 7 6 5 4 3 2 1

Contents

Illinois

Indiana

Acknowledgements

This book resulted from the extraordinary partnership between Rails-to-Trails Conservancy, Saturn Corporation, Hearst Magazines and Hal Riney & Partners. We are grateful to many people who made the relationship possible.

From Saturn, thanks to Don Hudler, Vice President, Sales/Marketing/Service; Steve Shannon, Director of Consumer Marketing; and Mary Wernette, National Advertising Manager.

From Hearst, we wish to thank Joe Kelly, Vice President and Managing Director; Carl Krampert, Detroit Group Manager; Lois Miller, Western Group Director; Jeanne O'Donnell, Group Director; John Kennelly, *Cosmopolitan*, New York Manager; and Janine Walters, *Cosmopolitan* San Francisco Manager.

From Hal Riney and Partners, thanks to Ellen Kiyomizu, Vice President, Associate Media Director; Kathleen Malone, Media Supervisor; Max Hegerman, Account Executive; and Doris Mitsch, Senior Writer.

Liz Elliott of Saturn and Holly Wernet of Hearst were our lead corporate contacts and deserve special recognition for enthusiastically answering hundreds of questions and for smoothly and efficiently overseeing this project.

We also offer a special thanks to Lisa McGimsey White and Bruce E. White of White & White, Inc., and to Daniel D'Arezzo, Deputy Editor of *Victoria* magazine.

Several individuals also need to be recognized for their contributions to this book.

Sharon Benjamin, Rails-to-Trails Conservancy's Vice President for Marketing, cultivated the relationship with Saturn and Hearst by maintaining constant communication and ensuring a high-quality final product. Her unwavering support and sense of humor kept us motivated throughout the entire project.

Greg Blanchard, Manager of Personnel and Technical Services for Rails-to-Trails Conservancy, overcame time crunches and technological difficulties to produce all of the maps included in this book.

Rah Trost receives a special note of thanks for keeping the Michigan Chapter running during the research phase of this book.

Special thanks to two contributing writers: Matthew L. Dickey, Director of Carmel/Clay (Indiana) Parks and Recreation, wrote the description of Indiana's Prairie-Duneland Trail and Rick Carey, President of the Blossomland River Trail Association in Niles, Michigan, wrote the description of Indiana's East Bank Trail.

Thanks also to the Boards of Directors for the Michigan and Illinois Chapters of Rails-to-Trails Conservancy for allowing the necessary time to do on-site trail research.

In addition, we would like to thank the trail managers who took the time to meet with us or to provide information we requested for some of the rail-trails included in this book.

In Michigan, thanks to John Gaffney of Copper Country State Forest; Duane St. Ours, Bill Nicholls and Hancock/Calumet Trails; Martin Nelson, Bergland to Sidnaw Trail; Russ McDonald, Felch Grade Trail; Amy Dover and Dick Anderson, Haywire Trail; Wayne Petterson, Little Falls Trail; Dennis Nezich, Republic/Champion Grade Trail; and Jerry Divine, State Line Trail.

In Illinois thanks to Steve Weller, McHenry County Prairie Trail (South); George Burrier, Rock Island Trail State Park; Audrey Friend, Long Prairie Trail; Bill Donnell, Virgil L. Gilman Nature Trail; and Martin Buehler, North Shore Bike Path.

In Indiana, thanks to Brian Creek, Bill Oliver and Dawn Hewitt of the Limestone Country Trail and Carl Fisher of the Prairie-Duneland Trail.

Roger Storm, Susan Wedzel,
Karen-Lee Ryan and Mike Ulm
March, 1994

Foreword

By now, you've probably noticed the Saturn logo on the cover of this book. And, if you have, you may be asking a very logical question: why would a car company want to sponsor a guide to a network of "roads" where you can't even drive?

Well, at Saturn, we feel very lucky to live and work in such a beautiful country. And, while we certainly want you to enjoy our cars, we also want you to be able to leave them in the garage now and then.

Which brings us to the subject of this book.

Before cars became our main mode of transportation, cities, towns, parks and forests all across America were connected by the most expansive railway system in the world. Nowadays, thousands of miles of rail corridors are abandoned every year—thousands of miles that pass through some of America's most amazing scenery and interesting places to visit. Fortunately, many of these empty railroad corridors are being converted to a different kind of transportation system.

Rail-trails are not only a beautiful way of preserving an important part of our country's history, they're also ideal for all kinds of sporting and outdoor activities, from walking to bicycling to cross-country skiing.

So we hope you'll take the time to explore a few of the rail-trails in this book—whether it's just for a little fresh air and exercise, to do some sightseeing or simply to get from point A to point B without using a drop of gasoline.

Who knows? Maybe you'll even be inspired to help preserve more rail-trails—in which case, Rails-to-Trails Conservancy would be delighted to hear from you.

In the meantime, let's hit the trail.

From the Saturn Team

Introduction

Welcome to an American adventure! Within these pages, you will find 40 unique experiences on America's fastest growing network of pathways to adventure: rail-trails.

Across the country, thousands of miles of former railroad corridors have been converted to trails for recreation, transportation and open space preservation. Whether you are a bicyclist, a walker, an equestrian, a wheelchair user, a cross-country skier, an in line skater or an outdoor enthusiast, rail-trails are for you!

Rail-trails traverse every conceivable environment from urban to suburban to rural, passing through farmland, river valleys, wetlands, residential areas, forests and lake shores. In metropolitan areas, rail-trails serve as linear parks that provide a respite from the hustle and bustle of everyday life. In rural areas, they run through some of the most scenic and pristine landscapes America has to offer.

The Midwest leads the nation in the number of rail-trails. In fact, with 60 rail-trails totaling more than 700 miles, Michigan has more rail-trails than any other state. Illinois, which has nearly 25 trails totaling more than 325 miles, is home to one of the first rail-trails—the Illinois Prairie Path. Indiana is following the lead of its neighboring states, opening several new trails in 1994 and undertaking a host of additional rail-trail projects.

The trails selected for *40 Great Rail-Trails in Michigan, Illinois and Indiana* offer surprising diversity and intriguing experiences for any trail user. New and exciting places await you on these trails— places where you can cross a river on bridges that span more than 1,200 feet, view some of the nation's only remaining native prairie plants, explore 140-foot-high sand dunes that are more than 3,500 years old, venture through areas logged and dammed by beavers, cut through steep limestone bluffs or visit a historical museum housed in a 120-year old railroad depot. These 40 great rail-trails will lead you to these places and many more.

History of the Rail-Trail Movement

In 1916, the United States was home to the world's most extensive railroad transportation network, with virtually every community connected together by routes of steel. At the pinnacle of the railroading era, nearly 300,000 miles of track spanned the nation— a network six times larger than today's interstate highway system.

Now, *less than half* of that original railroad network exists. Cars, trucks, buses and airplanes have led to the rapid decline of the railroad industry, which continues to abandon more than 2,000 miles of track every year.

The concept of preserving these valuable corridors and converting them into multi-use public trails began in the Midwest, where railroad abandonments were most widespread. Once the tracks came out, people naturally started using the corridors for walking and hiking while exploring railroad relics ranging from train stations and mills to bridges and tunnels.

While many people agreed with this great new concept, the reality of actually converting abandoned railroad corridors into public trails was a much greater challenge. From the late 1960s until the early 1980s, many rail-trail efforts failed as corridors were lost to development, sold to the highest bidder or broken up into many pieces.

In 1983, Congress enacted an amendment to the National Trails System Act directing the Interstate Commerce Commission to allow about-to-be abandoned railroad lines to be "railbanked," or set aside for future transportation use while being used as trails in the interim. In essence, this law preempts rail corridor abandonment, keeping the corridors intact for trail use and any possible future uses.

This powerful new piece of legislation made it easier for agencies and organizations to acquire rail corridors for trails, but many projects still failed because of short deadlines, lack of information and local opposition to trails.

In 1986, Rails-to-Trails Conservancy (RTC) formed to provide a national voice for the creation of rail-trails. RTC quickly developed a strategy to preserve the largest amount of rail corridor in the shortest period of time: a national advocacy program to defend the new railbanking law in the courts and in Congress, coupled with a direct project assistance program to help public agencies and local rail-trail groups overcome the challenges of converting a rail into a trail.

The strategy is working! In 1986, Rails-to-Trails Conservancy knew of only 75 existing rail-trails and 90 projects in the works. Today, there are more than 550 rail-trails and an additional 500 projects underway. The Rails-to-Trails Conservancy vision of creating an interconnected network of trails across the country is becoming a reality.

The thriving rails-to-trails movement has created nearly 7,000 miles of public trails for a wide range of users. And, in 1993, these rail-trails were used more than 86 million times. People all across the country are now realizing the incredible benefits of rail-trails.

Benefits of Rail-Trails

Rail-trails are flat or have gentle grades, making them perfect for multiple users, ranging from walkers and bicyclists to in-line skaters and people with disabilities. In snowy climates, they are ideal for cross-country skiing, snowmobiling and other snow activities. And, because of their length, they offer numerous access points.

In urban areas, rail-trails act as linear greenways through developed areas, efficiently providing much-needed recreation space while also serving as utilitarian transportation corridors. They link neighborhoods and workplaces and connect congested areas to open spaces. In many cities and suburbs, rail-trails are used for commuting to work, school and shopping.

In rural ares, rail-trails can provide a significant stimulus to local economies. People who use trails often spend money on food, beverages, camping, hotels, bed-and-breakfasts, bicycle rentals, souvenirs and other items. Studies have shown that trail users have generated as much as $1.25 million annually for the towns through which a trail passes.

Rail-trails preserve historic structures, such as train stations, bridges, tunnels, mills, factories and canals. These structures preserve an important piece of history and enhance the trail experience.

Wildlife viewing can also enhance the trail experience, and rail-trails are home to birds, plants, wetlands and a variety of small and

large mammals. Many rail-trails serve as plant and animal conservation corridors, and, in some cases, endangered species are located
along the route.

Recreation, transportation, historic preservation, economic re-
vitalization, open space conservation and wildlife preservation—
these are just some of the many benefits of rail-trails and the rea-
sons why people love them.

How to Get Involved

If you enjoy rail-trails, join the movement to save abandoned
rail corridors and to create more trails across the country. Donating
even a small amount of your time can help get more trails on the
ground.

◆ If you only have an hour, write a letter to your city, county or
state elected official in favor of pro rail-trail legislation. You could
also write a letter to the editor of your local newspaper praising a
trail or trail project. Or, you could attend a public hearing to voice
your support for a local trail, or send a letter to a friend sharing the
special qualities of rail-trails.

◆ If you have a day, volunteer to plant flowers or trees along an
existing trail or spend several hours helping out with a cleanup on a
nearby rail-trail project. Or, lead a hike along an abandoned corridor with your friends.

◆ If you have several hours a month, become an active member
in a trail effort in your area. Many groups host trail events, under-
take fundraising campaigns, publish brochures and newsletters and
carry out other activities to promote a trail or project. Virtually all
of these efforts are completed by volunteers, and they are always
looking for another helping hand.

Whatever your time allows, get involved! The success of a
community's rail-trail depends upon the level of citizen participa-
tion. Rails-to-Trails Conservancy can put you in touch with a local
group in your area. And, if you want to keep up on and support the
movement nationally, join Rails-to-Trails Conservancy. You will get
discounts on all RTC publications and merchandise, and you will be
supporting the largest national trails organization in the United
States. To become a member, use the order form at the back of this
book.

How to Use Rail-Trails

By design, rail-trails accommodate a variety of trail users. While this is generally one of the many benefits of rail-trails, it also can lead to occasional conflicts among trail users. Everyone should take responsibility to ensure trail safety by following a few simple trail etiquette guidelines.

One of the most basic etiquette rules is, "Wheels yield to heels." The figure below indicates the correct protocol for yielding right-of-way. Bicyclists (and in-line skaters) yield to other users; pedestrians yield to equestrians.

Generally, this means that you need to warn users (to whom you are yielding) of your presence. If, as a bicyclist, you fail to warn a walker that you are about to pass, the walker could step in front you, causing an accident that could have been prevented. Similarly, it is best to slow down and warn an equestrian of your presence. A horse can be startled by a bicycle, so make verbal contact with the rider and be sure it is safe to pass.

Here are some other guidelines you should follow to promote trail safety:

- Obey all trail-use rules posted at trailheads.
- Stay to the right except when passing
- Pass slower traffic on their left; yield to oncoming traffic when passing.
- Give a clear warning signal when passing; for example, call out, "Passing on your left."
- Always look ahead and behind when passing.
- Travel at a reasonable speed.
- Keep pets on a leash.
- Do not trespass on private property.
- Move off the trail surface when stopped to allow others to pass.
- Yield to other trail users when entering and crossing the trail.
- Do not disturb any wildlife.

How to Use This Book

At the beginning of each state, you will find a map showing the general location of each rail-trail listed in that state. The text description of every rail-trail begins with the following information:

Trail Name: The official name of the rail-trail is stated here.

Endpoints: This heading lists the endpoints for the entire trail, usually identified by a municipality or a nearby geographical point.

Location: The county or counties through which the trail passes are stated here.

Length: This indicates the length of the trail, including how many miles currently are open, and for those trails that are built partially on abandoned corridors, the number of miles actually on the rail line.

Surface: The materials that make up the surface of the rail-trail vary from trail to trail, and this heading describes each trail's surface, which ranges from asphalt and crushed stone to the significantly more rugged original railroad ballast.

Contact: The name, address and telephone number of each trail's manager are listed here. The selected contacts generally are responsible for managing the trail and can provide additional information about the trail and its condition.

Legend

In addition, every trail has a series of icons depicting uses allowed on the trail.

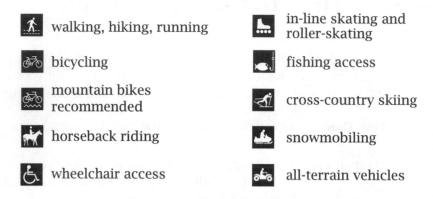

🚶	walking, hiking, running	🛼	in-line skating and roller-skating
🚲	bicycling	🎣	fishing access
🚵	mountain bikes recommended	⛷	cross-country skiing
🏇	horseback riding	🛷	snowmobiling
♿	wheelchair access	🚜	all-terrain vehicles

Uses permitted on individual trails are based on trail surfaces and are determined solely by trail managers. Rails-to-Trails Conservancy has no control over which uses are permitted and prohibited.

Wheelchair access is indicated for hard-surface trails. All trails that allow bicycling also allow mountain bicycling, but only on the trail surface—not in surrounding open areas. Trails that only list the mountain bicycling symbol have rougher terrains that are not suitable for road bikes. The all-terrain vehicle symbol generally does not include motorcycles and minibikes.

Map Legend

●	Trail endpoints	●	Cities and towns
▬▬▬	Rail-Trail	🛡94	Interstate highway
P	Parking	⬡10	U.S. highway
◆	Point of interest	⬡20	State Route

Rail-Trail Safety

The authors of this book have made every effort to ensure the accuracy of the information included here, however trails and their conditions can change at any time. It is your responsibility to ensure your own safety and exercise caution while using rail-trails, including knowing the limits of your own abilities and wearing a helmet when bicycling.

If you find inaccurate information or substantially different conditions, please send a letter detailing your findings to: Publications Department, Rails-to-Trails Conservancy, 1400 Sixteenth Street, NW, Washington, DC 20036.

An Introduction to Rail-Trails in Michigan

With 60 rail-trails, Michigan leads the nation as the state with the most trails created from abandoned rail corridors. This achievement provides safe and scenic places for individuals and families to recreate while preserving an important piece of Michigan's heritage.

The railroad industry played an important role in the development of the Great Lakes State, which was once home to nearly 10,000 miles of railroad tracks. Today, only 4,500 miles remain active. Fortunately, interested citizens took the lead in the 1970s and 1980s to preserve these corridors by supporting local trail projects, such as the Paint Creek Trail near Rochester, the Kal-Haven Trail near Kalamazoo, the LakeLands Trail near Jackson and the Hart-Montague Trail near Muskegon.

In 1985, several trail user groups got together and agreed to form a statewide organization to share information and to promote their common interest in rail-trails. The group, incorporated as the Michigan TRRails Alliance, became the Michigan Chapter of Rails-to-Trails Conservancy in 1988. With a two-staff office in Lansing, the Michigan Chapter works to get more rail-trails on the ground by providing technical assistance to agencies and local trail groups, working with elected officials and promoting the rail-trail movement throughout the state.

All of the hard work is paying off, as new trails open and others are extended. The ultimate goal is to develop an interconnected state-wide trail system—known as the Discover Michigan Trail—that links together communities, parks, historic sites and the Great Lakes.

This book will offer you a glimpse into why an interconnected network would create an exceptional resource. From the rugged experience of the trails in the Upper Peninsula to the new generation of surfaced trails in the Lower, the 25 rail-trails chosen for this book typify Michigan's wonderful heritage and diversity. Enjoy!

Special Considerations for Upper Peninsula Trails

Keep in mind that conditions on individual trails can change with the seasons, and this is particularly true of rail-trails in Michigan's Upper Peninsula. You could have a completely different experience than what is described in this book. The Upper Peninsula rail-trails were developed primarily as part of Michigan's snowmobile trail network, and bicycling on these unrefined trails requires a mountain bike—the wider the tires, the better. Finally, remember that the Upper Peninsula trails allow motorized users. While such use is generally light, don't be surprised if an occasional off-road vehicle passes you.

MICHIGAN'S GREAT RAIL-TRAILS

1. Baw Beese Trail
2. Bergland to Sidnaw Trail
3. Bill Nicholls Trail
4. Boardwalk of Grand Haven
5. Crossroads Trail
6. Felch Grade Trail
7. Frank N. Andersen Trail
8. Hancock/Calumet Trail
9. Hart-Montague Trail State Park
10. Haywire Trail
11. Kal-Haven Sesquicentennial Trail State Park
12. Kent Trails
13. Kiwanis Trail
14. LakeLands Trail State Park
15. Little Falls Trail
16. Little Traverse Wheelway
17. Mackinaw/Alanson Trail
18. Nordhouse Dunes Trail System
19. Paint Creek Trail
20. Pere Marquette Rail-Trail of Mid-Michigan
21. Republic/Champion Grade Trail
22. State Line Trail
23. Traverse Area Recreational Trail (TART)
24. Watersmeet/Land O'Lakes Trail
25. West Bloomfield Trail Network

Baw Beese Trail

Endpoints: Sandy Beach on Baw Beese Lake to Lake Pleasant Road east of Hillsdale

Location: Hillsdale County

Length: 2.2 miles (will be 6 miles when completed)

Surface: Dirt, gravel, cinder and original ballast

Uses:

Contact: Mark Reynolds, Recreation Director
43 McCollum
Hillsdale, MI 49242
517-437-3579

◆◆◆

Named in honor of Chief Baw Beese of the Potawatomi Indians, beautiful Baw Beese Lake serves as the setting for the historic Baw Beese Trail.

Starting on the north shore of the lake, the trail travels down one of Michigan's oldest railroad corridors—one of two rail lines planned and partially built by the state soon after statehood was granted in 1836. The railroad arrived in Hillsdale in 1843, and soon thereafter was incorporated as the Michigan Southern Railroad Company.

Abandoned by Penn Central Railroad in 1976, vegetation is slowly reclaiming the corridor: small trees now grow right up to the old grade. The trail surface is unimproved and consists mainly of gravel and cinder. Designated part of the route for the North Country National Scenic Trail, future plans call for the Baw Beese Trail to be extended into the City of Hillsdale.

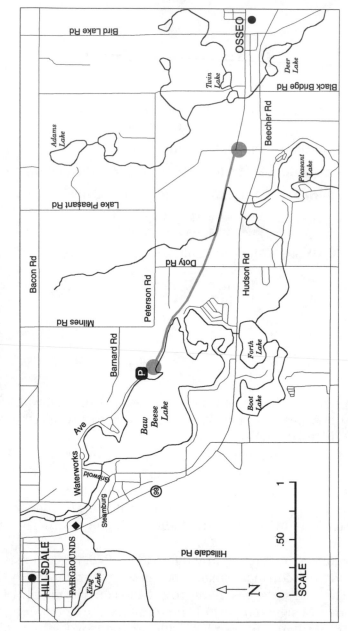

BAW BEESE TRAIL

Trotting along the Baw Beese Trail

To find the trail, take Michigan State Route 99 (M-99) south of Hillsdale and turn east on Steamburg Road, just south of the fairgrounds. Go past the Orville E. Meyer Parkway, where the road will swing right; go behind a cemetery and turn left on Griswold Street. Turn right on Water Works Avenue and head east toward Baw Beese Lake. You will pass several parks along the lake on your right, where parking is available. To your left you will see the abandoned rail corridor proposed for future development.

The closest parking (0.3 miles from the trail) is at Sandy Beach. Follow the dirt road along the lake. When you reach the bollards—posts that prevent motorized vehicles on the trail—you are at the trailhead. Have a seat on the bench, kick back, relax and enjoy the view.

Agate Falls, under the trestle on the Middle Branch of the Ontonagon River

Bergland to Sidnaw Trail

Endpoints: East of Bergland to Sidnaw

Location: Houghton and Ontonagon Counties

Length: 43 miles

Surface: Dirt, gravel, sand and original ballast

Uses:

Contact: Martin Nelson, Area Forest Manager
Copper Country State Forest
P. 0. Box 440
Baraga, MI 49908
906-353-6651

◆◆◆

There's no need to hold your breath along this trail while teetering across steep land bridges or crossing the extensive bridges that tower over streams and rivers—the spectacular views will take your breath away.

You will reach the highlight of your trip about midway through this 43-mile trail as you overlook Agate Falls rushing down the rocky steps of the Middle Branch of the Ontonagon River. All this while the trail follows, but somehow eludes, Michigan State Route 28.

The Bergland to Sidnaw Trail starts a couple of miles east of Bergland, but unfortunately, no parking is available at the trailhead. The Bergland Township Park on Lake Gogebic, which is about two miles from the trail, offers the best starting point. From the park, head north on Ash to M-28, then turn right. The road has a wide shoulder to ease the trip to East Shore Road, which is an eroded, washed-out two-track that you will spot after passing sewage disposal ponds on your right. Turn right and travel a half-mile to the

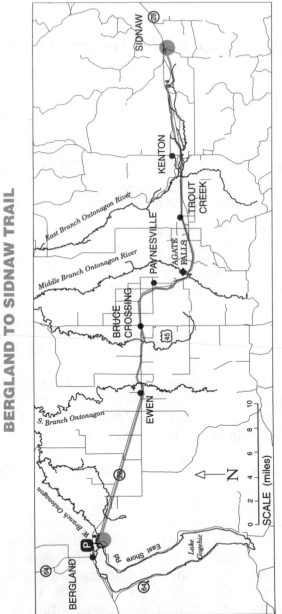

BERGLAND TO SIDNAW TRAIL

trail, where you will turn left and embark on the first leg of your journey.

The 12.5-mile stretch to Ewen is pretty coarse. Recently relinquished from rail use, the corridor is heavily laden with ballast, and the young vegetation is not ample enough to make this portion of the trail particularly scenic. An occasional stand of more stately trees and several beaver huts help keep the trail interesting. The trail also has some fierce gravel spots, so some mountain bikers may want to ride the roadway (M-28) or just begin the trip in Ewen.

Less than a quarter-mile out of Ewen (before you cautiously cut across M-28), you will pass the first impressive bridge as it spans the South Branch of the Ontonagon River. Continue along past birch trees, over a long land bridge and past drives and roads to the second expansive bridge. Once over the Baltimore River, you are about one mile from crossing M-45 at Bruce Crossing.

For the next seven miles, you will travel over land bridges and wet areas and past farm and pasture lands. You will also cut through the small town of Paynesville before entering the hardwoods and pines that promote your approach to Agate Falls. Stop and take a few short breaths (and maybe some pictures) before embarking on this long, lofty bridge.

While the view from the bridge is impressive, the falls tend to look like a flat, two-dimensional photo. For added dimension, take the steep path down after you cross the bridge and experience the full depth of the falls as the water cascades past you. (You can also reach this area by stopping at the rest area off State Route 28, then walking along a short path that takes you under the bridge and down to the falls.)

Back up to the trail (gasping for air), continue along for about four miles into Trout Creek. Here you can find sanctuary in a historical museum that is home to a steam engine display. In another four miles, you will cross a jumbo bridge over the Jumbo River. Continue on past pines and ferns, before curving onto the last large bridge past Kenton. Sparrow Park is to your right if you feel like a picnic.

Intermittent ballast and gravel make for rough traveling over the next five or six miles, followed by enjoyable woods, wet areas and land bridges—don't look down the slopes if you are afraid of heights. You will reach the trail's eastern terminus in Sidnaw, where the trail ends at Erie Street. If you look ahead, you can see where the corridor forks into an active rail line.

Michigan Snowmobile Trail System

Beginning with the passage of the Snowmobile Act in 1968, the snowmobile trail system has grown to a statewide network of more than 4,800 miles of groomed trails located on state, federal and private lands. An additional 15,000 miles of ungroomed forest roads also are open to snowmobiling.

Combining the trail system with snowfalls ranging from 60 inches to more than 200 inches and average temperatures around 20 degrees, Michigan's Upper Peninsula is snowmobile heaven. Trails literally crisscross the peninsula, making it possible for snowmobilers to go from one end of the U.P. to the other without ever leaving their machines.

Without the snowmobile trail program, very few abandoned rail corridors ever would have been purchased in the Upper Peninsula—trails that are now available for multiple uses during warmer months.

Snowmobilers tour the spectacular winter scenery along the Upper Peninsula trails.

Bill Nicholls Trail

Endpoints: Houghton to Adventure Mountain, north of Mass City

Location: Houghton and Ontonagon Counties

Length: 40.5 miles

Surface: Dirt, gravel, sand and original ballast

Uses:

Contact: Martin Nelson
Area Forest Manager
Copper Country State Forest
P. O. Box 440
Baraga, MI 49908
906-353-6651

◆ ◆ ◆

I f you are looking for a rail-trail that is scenic and challenging, this could be the trail for you. After all, how many rail-trails have Adventure Mountain as a trailhead?

Abandoned in 1972 by the Copper Range Railroad, this corridor has served primarily as a snowmobile trail since its acquisition by the Department of Natural Resources in 1974. The trail begins on Canal Drive, west of downtown Houghton, and parking is available at Veramize Park (south of the trail) along the Portage Lake Ship Canal. From the park, go up the hill on Lake Avenue and turn right on Canal Drive, which has a marked, paved shoulder on both sides. The trail starts on the south side of the road.

This first section, paralleling the road, is a bit overgrown and rocky with uphill slopes. After about a mile, you reach a point where

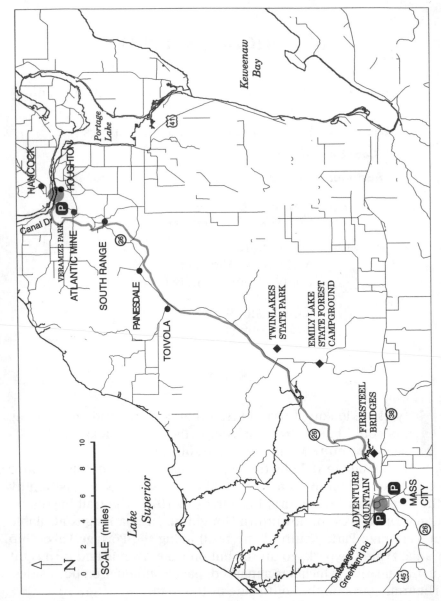

BILL NICHOLLS TRAIL

a large bridge has been removed. A stone surface leads you down to the road and back up to the trail on the other side. The slope is steep and the stone is loose, so use caution—walk your bike if you have one.

The trail turns south about a half-mile later, where a scenic over-look offers views of the Portage Lake Ship Canal. Beyond the over-look, the trail continues to climb for another 2.5 miles, and a host of railroad ties still entrenched in the trail's surface may jar your bones at times. After passing a cemetery on your left, you will cross your first road since the missing bridge before approaching some houses.

A mile beyond the houses the trail splits and you should stay to the right. The trail splits again 0.3 mile later, at a location known as Mill Mine Junction. Here, you veer to the left. The trail to the right, known as the Freda Trail, is open only in the winter for snowmobile use.

For the next mile, sand periodically clogs the trail, until you reach a sign over the trail welcoming you to the community of South Range. This town offers various services, most of which appear listed on the sign over the trail.

A couple of miles south of South Range, outside the community of Painesdale, the trail enters an area heavily impacted by mining activities. The trail passes old ruins and mine tailings, as well as an old Copper Range Railroad rail car. At one point, the trail again has a bridge missing. Mountain bicyclists may want to walk their bikes down and up the steep slopes. When you reach the top, take the road to the right, go over a small bridge and then immediately turn left to get back on the trail. Here, you will be paralleling a new service road on your right. The trail continues past another old mining operation and through a tunnel of trees. Then, with a tower as your beacon, you arrive at the community of Toivola, which offers a restaurant and a small grocery store, nearly nine miles outside of South Range.

From Toivola to the State Park at Twin Lakes—about eight miles—the trail passes several small lakes, traverses scenic woodlands and is periodically lined with wild blackberry and thimbleberry bushes. The trail surface, while generally ridable, is often soft and loose. The trail parallels M-26 for several miles, allowing easy access to nearby businesses that cater to park users and also to Twin Lakes State Park, which offers camping.

Scenic overlook of the Portage Lake Ship Canal

Leaving the state park, the trail continues for about 15.5 miles to the trailhead at Adventure Mountain. Near the park, the trail parallels M-26 for a few miles, where the surface gives way to sand and bumps in several locations. After crossing M-26, you will enter the trail's most scenic section, which stretches nearly 11 miles. The highlights include crossing the Firesteel River on three successive steel bridges that total 1,288 feet in length and have a maximum clearance over the water of 80 feet. The decking on the bridges is primitive at best, so bicyclists should walk across and enjoy the view.

After crossing the bridges, the real adventure begins. The trail crosses M-38 less than two miles after the last bridge and then splits a half-mile later. Stay to the RIGHT, although it looks as if you should go to the left. This section is quite rugged. After you hit a stretch of trail that has railroad ties for its surface, look for a sign that points you to the right. From here the trail goes cross-country for 1.5 miles to the trailhead at Adventure Mountain. This rugged section is very hilly, and may be more than most people would care to tackle.

Alternative end routes include:

◆ No Adventure: turn right when you reach M-38, head north to M-26 and turn left. Turn left again at the junction of M-26 and M-38, and follow M-26 south to Mass City, where you will find a park-and-ride lot and places to eat and sleep.

◆ Some Adventure: turn left when you get to M-26 after completing the first half of the cross-country ride to Adventure Mountain. Follow M-26 south to Mass City.

Boardwalk of Grand Haven

Endpoints: Second Street to the Grand Haven Lighthouse in the City of Grand Haven

Location: Ottawa County

Length: .75 mile of a 2.5-mile trail is on an abandoned rail corridor

Surface: Asphalt and wood planks

Uses: 🚶 🚴 ♿ ⛸

Contact: Teresa Jones or Laurel Nease
Grand Haven Visitors Bureau
One South Harbor Drive
Grand Haven, MI 49417
616-842-4499

◆ ◆ ◆

Strolling down the Boardwalk of Grand Haven, you will be captivated by the sights and sounds of this revitalized area. Shops, eateries, boats on the Grand River and people walking or resting along the landscaped parks fill the area that once operated as many as 90 trains a day.

Beginning east of the Farmers Market on Harbor Drive (where parking is available), a self-guided tour wanders past a collection of railroad artifacts. Here the historic Pere Marquette Steam Locomotive #1223 and several restored rail cars and cabooses join the 79-foot-high Grand Trunk Western Standard Coaling Tower as relics (and reminders) of a bygone era.

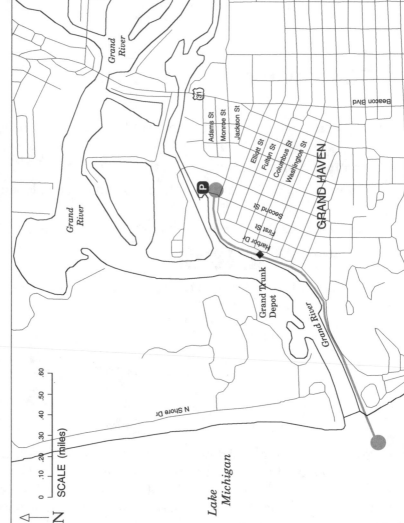

Heading west from the Farmers Market is Chinook Pier, which features a vast array of shops and restaurants. The pier also is the home of the Harbor Steamer tour boat, numerous charter fishing boats and a miniature golf course.

Continuing along the river past the City Marina you will see the 2,400-seat Waterfront Stadium. Built primarily for viewing the summertime performances of the "World's Largest Musical Fountain," the stadium also hosts other local, live performances.

Behind the stadium is the Tri-Cities Historical Museum, housed in the old railroad depot constructed by the Detroit, Grand Haven and Milwaukee Railroad in 1870. Originally the railroad ended on the other side of the Grand River, and for 12 years, passengers had to take a ferry into town.

As Grand Haven grew to become a major transportation terminal, the rail yards grew to contain all the facilities needed to serve the railroads. These included a six-stall engine house with a turntable, a grain elevator, an ice house, the coaling tower, a car ferry slip and a 400-foot warehouse where the Waterfront Stadium now stands.

Immediately upon leaving the museum, you will pass the William Ferry Landing, where the first permanent settler landed with his family. The memorial embedded in the walkway is a brass replica (to scale) of the Grand River.

From here you leave the land where trains once ruled, and proceed to Lake Michigan. The Boardwalk continues along Bicentennial Park, past Government Pond, through Escanaba Park, beside Grand Haven State Park and on to the Grand Haven south pier. Walking along the south pier in the shadow of its catwalk takes you out to the historic Grand Haven Lighthouse. Take your time and enjoy the view the sunsets are spectacular.

Dusk settles over the boardwalk.

Walkers enjoy the Crossroads Trail's new surface.

Crossroads Trail

Endpoints: Roth Road to Patterson Road in Reed City

Location: Osceola County

Length: 1 mile, eventually will be part of the 54-mile Clare to Baldwin Trail

Surface: Asphalt

Uses: 🚶 🚴 ♿ ⛸ ⛷

Contact: William Porteous, Chair
Crossroads Trail Committee
8511 Walnut Drive
Reed City, MI 49677
616-832-9869

❖ ❖ ❖

I f, as the saying goes, all journeys start with a single step, then the Reed City Crossroads Trail Committee recently took a huge one. Using only private donations, the group successfully completed a one-mile demonstration trail on the abandoned east-west corridor through Reed City.

The asphalt trail is intended to serve the needs of the local community. Stretching from Patterson Road to Roth Street, the trail provides access to downtown Reed City and, in the future, will link to the community's existing Linear Park along the Hersey River.

Eventually, Reed City will benefit from its unique position at the crossroads of two recreational rail-trails. The Michigan Department of Natural Resources already has purchased the 54-mile corridor from Clare to Baldwin and is negotiating with the Department of Transportation to purchase a 92-mile corridor from Grand Rapids to Cadillac.

CROSSROADS TRAIL

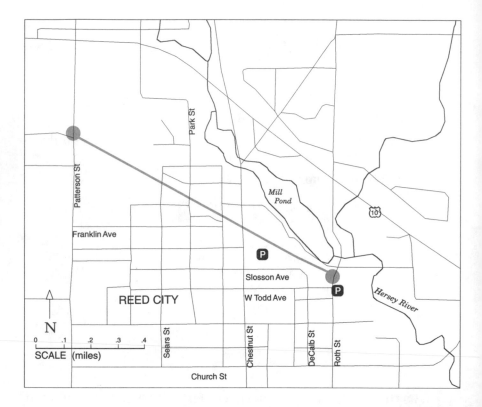

As completion of the one-mile trail shows, members of the Reed City Crossroads Trail Committee did not want to wait for all this to happen. They went forward, took the first step of their journey, and rolled out the welcome mat (read: asphalt) not only to the people within their community, but also to welcome other people *to* their community.

Diamond Memorial

The intact version of the diamond crossing

The future looks brighter for the old diamond-shaped rail crossing at Reed City. Cast aside when salvagers pulled up the tracks
and ties, the crossing is now stored in a Michigan Department
of Transportation garage. Originally known as the diamond
crossing, Ferris State University students are designing a more
fitting tribute for the crossing—a Diamond Memorial—which
will be prominently located along the Crossroads Trail as a
reminder of the area's railroad heritage.

A view of a meadow reclaiming barn from the Felch Grade Trail

Felch Grade Trail

Endpoints: Felch to west of Escanaba

Location: Dickinson, Menominee, and Delta Counties

Length: 40 miles, plus an additional 5 miles off-grade only open to snowmobiling

Surface: Dirt, gravel, sand and original ballast

Uses:

Contact: Russ McDonald
Escanaba River State Forest
1126 North Lincoln Road
Escanaba, MI 49829
906-786-2354

◆◆◆

I t is not always easy to describe the rail-trail experience to some-
one new to the concept. The perception people have of a trail
corridor from a passing car is quite different from the reality
of actually using that same corridor as a trail. Rail-trails must be
experienced to be understood; the Felch Grade Trail is the perfect
example.

For two-thirds of its length, this trail parallels Michigan State
Route 69—right along the highway, in fact. From the road, the trail
might not look like anything special. But from the trail, your awareness of the lightly-traveled road is masked by the vegetation that
has grown since the corridor was abandoned in 1970. And, most
likely, you will be surprised by the amazing number of white-tailed
deer using the trail as a travel route.

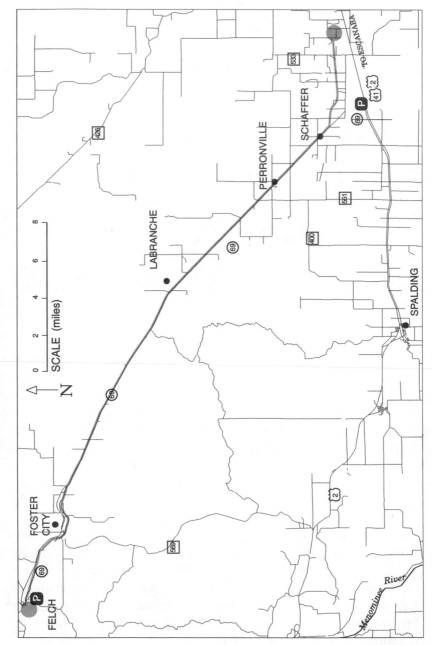

FELCH GRADE TRAIL

White-Tailed Deer

With an estimated 1.7 million white-tailed deer, Michigan has the second largest population in the country, behind Texas. Since deer's natural predators of wolf, cougar, coyote and lynx have dwindled in numbers, deer abound in Michigan. During the summer in the Upper Peninsula, deer may be the most frequent rail-trail users!

Lacking upper incisors, deer tear vegetation away from branches or from the ground. Adult deer eat about 10 pounds of food per day during the growing season and eat what they can find in the winter.

Their coats also change with the seasons. Reddish-brown in the summer (with spots on the young), their coats turn bark-brown or grayish in the winter. Common to all seasons is the white rump and the identifying white tail underneath. When a deer is alarmed, it raises its tail, swishes it back and forth and bounds off—usually with what sounds like a sneeze, a noise made when they exhale loudly through their nostrils.

Deer usually start looking for food about an hour before sunset and continue until about an hour after sunrise. They are especially active in the fall, which is the rutting season. Gestation usually takes about 200 days, so most young are born in late May or early June.

Two white-tailed deer taking a dip.

In the end, you may be relieved that M-69 is so near, as the Felch Grade Trail is extremely rough, and occasionally proves to be more than some users can handle.

The trail begins in the community of Felch. You can park near the swing sets behind the Felch Township Community Center on M-69. To get to the trail, take Andy's Lane from behind the Community Center, turn right on Van Lear Drive and left on Old Dump Road. After two blocks, turn left and then make a right onto the trail.

The first 7.7 miles, from Felch to M-69, is scenic and wet. The trail passes through wetlands, crosses a corner of the Copper Country State Forest and runs along a branch of the Sturgeon River and the two creeks that feed into it. South of Foster City, the trail briefly merges with a dirt road. Where the trail is overgrown, you can ride a short stretch of a parallel dirt road.

After crossing M-69, the trail runs along the east side of the highway for the next 26.4 miles. You've reached the trail's halfway point when you get to LaBranche, which offers a store and a tavern. Other stops along this stretch occur at Perronville and Schafer. At Perronville, about 8.5 miles from LaBranche, a pathway has been cleared to provide access to a small store and pub. From here it is just another 3.6 miles to a grocery store in Schafer.

One mile south of Schaffer, after crossing an active rail line, the trail takes an interesting turn, where three rail lines once crossed this junction. The Felch Grade railroad continued straight for two more miles, where it fed into another rail line. Veering left, the trail now leaves that corridor and continues for another six miles on what was a different rail line. The red trail surface here is in better shape than the rest of the trail.

One highlight along this section is the bridge over the Ford River, unfortunately, there is no parking at this end, but one possibility is to use the park-and-ride lot at M-69 and U.S. 2. From here you go north on M-69 for about a mile, to County Road 521, where you can pickup the old Felch Grade. Or, continue on M-69 for another 1.2 miles to the junction.

Frank N. Andersen Nature Trail

Endpoints: Jenison Nature Center in the Bay City State Park to Tobico Marsh Trail Observation Tower

Location: Bay County

Length: 1 mile, .65 miles on an abandoned rail corridor

Surface: asphalt and gravel

Uses:

Contact: Karen Gillispie
Bay City State Park
3582 State Park Drive
Bay City, MI 48706
517-684-3020

❖ ❖ ❖

Linking the Jenison Nature Center at the Bay City State Park to the Tobico Marsh State Game Area, this is one nature trail that is bicycle friendly. The trail has an asphalt surface on the old rail grade and bike racks at the nature observation decks. The bike racks help keep the trail clear of visitors enjoying the wildlife.

After leaving the nature center (open Wednesday through Sunday, 10 a.m. to 4 p.m.), the trail heads north into a wooded area, where the first of the observation decks awaits you. The decks are covered wooden shelters with benches and interpretive plaques featuring plants and animals found in that particular habitat. The first one features the trees and birds that might be found here in the woodland zone. Leaving the woods, the trail enters a large marsh

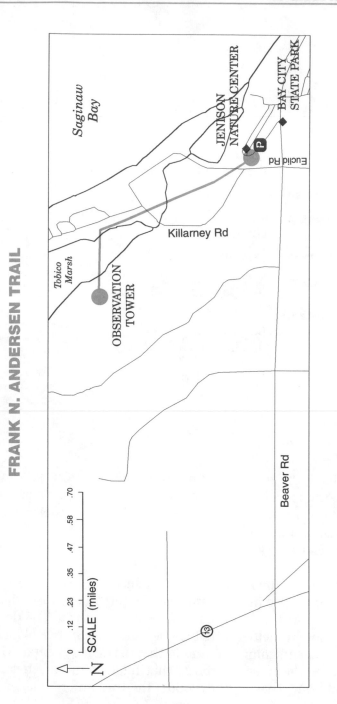

FRANK N. ANDERSEN TRAIL

Saginaw Bay

JENISON NATURE CENTER

BAY CITY STATE PARK

Euclid Rd

Killarney Rd

Tobico Marsh

OBSERVATION TOWER

Beaver Rd

N

SCALE (miles)

0   .12   .23   .35   .47   .58   .70

Strolling along the Frank N. Andersen Nature Trail

area, where the second observation deck highlights marsh plants and animals.

Shortly after crossing a road, the trail turns left off the rail grade, where the trail becomes gravel and cuts across a large wetland with numerous interpretive stops. Keep an eye on the water—you might get lucky and spot a beaver.

Once across the wetland, you arrive at a large, two-story observation tower overlooking the marsh. If you want to extend your visit, you can pick up the Tobico Marsh Trail from near the base of the tower.

There is no fee to use the nature trail, but a daily or annual vehicle permit is required to enter the Bay City State Park.

A bridge along the Hancock/Calumet Trail—not decked for bicyclists.

Hancock/Calumet Trail

Endpoints: Old depot in Calumet to Poorvoo Park in Hancock

Location: Houghton County

Length: 13 miles

Surface: Dirt, gravel, sand, cinder and original ballast

Uses:

Contact: Martin Nelson, Area Forest Manager
Copper Country State Forest
P. O. Box 440
Baraga, MI 49908
906-353-6651

❖ ❖ ❖

uilt in 1908 by the Mineral Range Railroad, the Calumet Depot once served as the point of entry to Calumet for thousands of immigrant mine workers and their families. Today, boarded up and showing signs of neglect, the depot stands not only as a reminder of a time gone by, but also as a logical starting point from which to enjoy this trail.

The depot can be found at the intersection of 9th and Oak Streets on the western edge of Calumet's Historic Business District. While parking is available here, no signs indicate that parking is allowed or even that a trail exists. Beginning at the depot, you will head south. After traveling a quarter of a mile, you pass under a bridge that once carried the trains of the Calumet & Hecla Railroad. The bridge, now idle, silently stands as a gateway to Calumet for trail users. Just south of the bridge the trail enters wetlands and passes

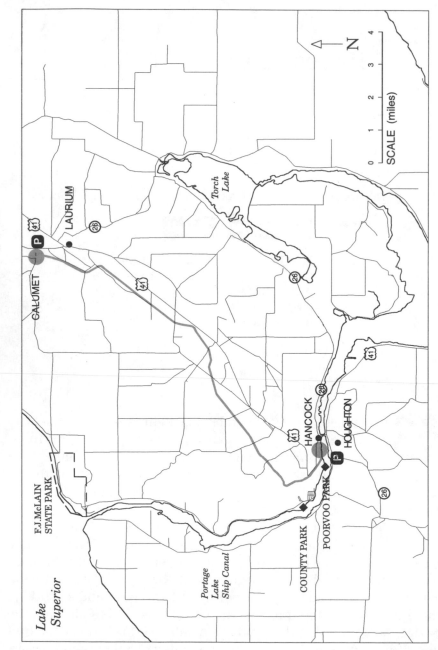

HANCOCK/CALUMET TRAIL

Lake Superior

F.J.McLAIN STATE PARK

Portage Lake Ship Canal

COUNTY PARK

POORVOO PARK

HANCOCK

HOUGHTON

CALUMET

LAURIUM

Torch Lake

N

SCALE (miles)
0 1 2 3 4

the Swedetown Pond and Swedetown Pathway, followed by Swedetown. Periodically you will see a relic of the mining era.

Abandoned by the Soo Line in 1979, this rail corridor has been ripe for new vegetative growth that adds a natural feel to the trail experience. Although the surface tends to feel soft and spongy at times, the trail is generally ridable by a mountain bike. However, it is a good idea to walk bikes across the bridges.

As you approach the Hancock Area, the trail will veer to the left and slope down—a steep descent for a rail grade. Erosion has exposed large rocks and left small gullies within the trail surface, making this section tough to negotiate. A brief respite occurs when the trail merges with U.S. 41, where, a paved shoulder has been built. It provides a couple blocks of smooth surface before the trail veers away from the road to the right. Be careful, you may be coasting at such a fast speed that you miss the arrow for the trail.

From this point, the trail continues for about another half-mile to the trailhead at Poorvoo Park, located on the Portage Lake Ship Canal at the base of Tezcuco Street in Hancock. The park has a small shelter with picnic tables, restrooms, a small boat dock and some parking. A wooden stairway also has been constructed to an observation deck on the bluff. As you look south across the ship canal, and just a little to the right, you may see where you can access the Bill Nicholls Trail. If you want to extend your trip, cross the lift bridge and continue on the Bill Nicholls Trail (see page 23).

Training for the upcoming ski season

Hart-Montague Bicycle Trail
State Park

Endpoints: Hart to Montague

Location: Oceana and Muskegon Counties

Length: 22.5 miles

Surface: Asphalt

Uses:

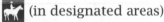 (in designated areas)

Contact: Peter Lundborg
Silver Lake State Park
Route 1, Box 254
Mears, MI 49436
616-873-3083

◆◆◆

T he Hart-Montague Trail holds a special place in the hearts of many Michiganians since it is often the first rail-trail they experience, and it is the first state park rail-trail with an improved surface.

John Gurney Park in the City of Hart is considered the trail's northern trailhead. The city portion of the route winds past Hart Lake and follows city streets west and south to the old grade at the corner of Wood and Water Streets. From here the trail is uphill for about a half-mile to the parking area on Polk Road, where most people begin on the trail's northern end. Across the street you will see the state park portion, highlighted by the first of many mile-markers.

HART-MONTAGUE BICYCLE TRAIL STATE PARK

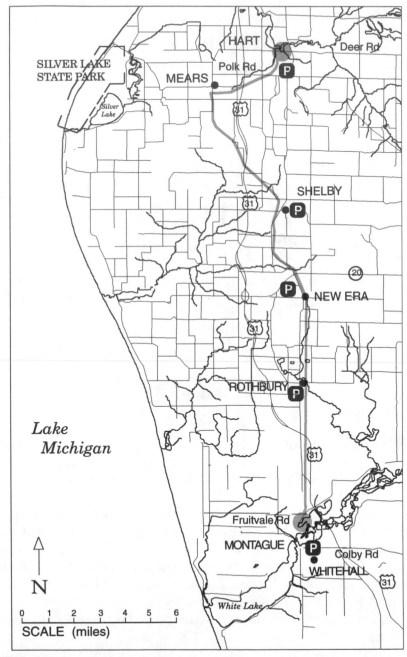

A new scenic rest stop overlooks East Golden Pond.

This trail will take you through a pleasant mix of forests, orchards, farmland and small communities. From Hart to Mears, you will head southwest, passing asparagus fields, orchards and woods until you pass under U.S. 31.

This short section was not part of the original rail line. When the Chicago and Michigan Lake Shore Railroad constructed the line in 1872, it went north to Pentwater. It was not until 10 years later that the railroad built a spur to Hart on land donated by its citizens. As you head south out of Mears, the trail will curve to the left. Here, you can still see evidence of the old line that ran north to Pentwater.

Bill Field—Father of the Hart-Montague Trail

Bill Field at an event along the Hart-Montague Trail.

After taking his family on Wisconsin's rail-trails, Bill Field proposed in 1981 that the abandoned rail corridor between Hart and Montague be converted into a multi-use trail. While intense local discussions took place between trail supporters and opponents, Field decided to buy the corridor with $175,000 of his own money to preserve the corridor until the matter was resolved.

The dedication of Field and other trail proponents led to growing local support, eventually leading to all of the surrounding communities' support for the trail. The trail's turning point came in 1987 when the City of Hart stepped forward as the trail project's local governmental agency sponsor. This made it possible for Field, who had sold some excess property along the route to recoup his investment, to deed the property to the City of Hart, which immediately deeded the property to the Michigan Department of Natural Resources in 1988. The trail was completed in 1990.

For his efforts leading to the creation of the Hart-Montague Trail, Bill Field was one of 15 named "Michiganians of the Year" for 1988 by the Detroit News' MICHIGAN magazine. The award honored "people who made this state a better place because of things they did in 1988."

From Mears to Shelby is perhaps the trail's most scenic stretch—two rest stops are provided for your viewing enjoyment. The newest is near the Mile 4 post, where a deck has been built overlooking East Golden Pond. The scenic view from the second stop, less than two miles away, has been depicted on Rails-to-Trails Conservancy note cards. Back on the trail, you will go under U.S. 31 again, past the Shelby Industrial Park (where you can see gems made) and into the Village of Shelby. A large picnic shelter with restrooms has been built near the old depot and parking is available.

Leaving Shelby, the trail parallels old U.S. 31 for roughly four miles, and near the Mile 11 post it crosses the only trestle along the entire route. The Village of New Era has developed a trailside park complete with a picnic area, parking and a covered pavilion that includes restrooms and a small creek. In addition, a small wood chip trail leads to an ice cream parlor.

South of New Era, the trail straightens out for several miles until it jogs around a parking lot in Rothbury. The town has developed a side-trail to a local park that offers a picnic area and a pavilion with restrooms and a playground.

Leaving Rothbury, the trail continues its beeline south and briefly runs through property of the Manistee National Forest. Near Mile 18, the trail goes under U.S. 31 for the third time. Several miles later you will veer to the right, signaling that you are near the trail's end. At the Montague trailhead, parking is available along Stanton Street (across from the Bicycle Depot bike shop), although parking lot construction is scheduled in 1994.

This is a state park that requires a user pass. Trail passes, which are a major source of revenue for trail operations, can be purchased at various businesses in the communities along the route or from the park rangers patrolling the trail. Individual daily passes are $2 and annual passes are $10. Family daily passes cost $5 and annual family passes cost $25. Passes purchased on the Hart-Montague Trail are valid on other state park rail-trails.

Boardwalk over the Indian River at the trailhead near Manistique

Beavers have created their own "home sweet home" along the trail.

Haywire Trail

Endpoints: South of Shingleton to Manistique

Location: Alger and Schoolcraft Counties

Length: 33 miles

Surface: Dirt, gravel, sand and original ballast

Uses: 🚶 🚵 🐎 🛷 🚜

Contacts: Dick Anderson, Assistant Ranger
Munising Ranger District
Hiawatha National Forest
RR2, Box 400
Munising, MI 49862
906-387-2512

Amy Dover, Area Fire Supervisor
Shingleton Forest Area
Lake Superior State Forest
M-28
Shingleton, MI 49884
906-452-6227

◆◆◆

You're in beaver country, so plan on getting your feet wet. This adventurous rail-trail wanders through miles of wetlands, crosses over 14 small bridges (but only six roads) and plows through a few merciless sand traps. Those undaunted by the occasional washout or water over the trail will be rewarded, not only with wet shoes and socks, but also by the serenity of the Hiawatha National and Lake Superior State Forests through which the trail meanders.

HAYWIRE TRAIL

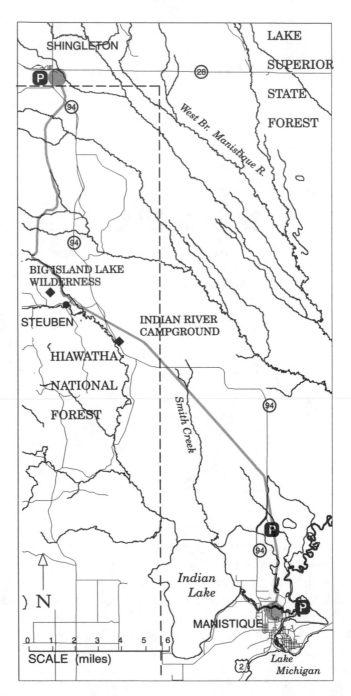

While you can navigate the wet trail without a ferry, ferries played an important role in the corridor's past. After the rail-line was constructed in 1902, the Ann Arbor Railroad began to ferry railcars to Manistique from Frankfort. The Ann Arbor had made railroad history 10 years earlier by becoming the first company to operate a railcar ferry across open water.

Abandoned after 66 years, this corridor may have become Michigan's first rail-trail when Schoolcraft County purchased it in the late 1960s. In 1970, the U.S. Forest Service and the Department of Natural Resources purchased it from the county and continued operating the route as a trail.

After the corridor was purchased, part of it was reserved to maintain access to the active east-west rail line at Shingleton. This made it necessary to cut a 0.3-mile connector from the corridor to M-94 to establish a trailhead. A sign marks this northern trailhead on the east side of State Route 94 just south of Shingleton. There is no parking, but spaces are available east of the Tanglewood Restaurant and Antique Shop on M-28 in Shingleton less than a quarter mile north of the trail.

Angling toward the old railgrade, the first 0.3 mile has ruts and may be seasonally wet. Mountain bikers should be prepared to walk. An alternative for some is to stay on M-94 (which has a three-foot paved shoulder) for 1.3 miles and pick up the trail where it first crosses the highway. From this point it is 11.6 miles to Steuben, which has a small convenience store and a few cabins. Steuben is the only area resembling a community between Shingleton and Manistique, so make sure that you are carrying an adequate supply of drinking water.

If you are traveling by mountain bike, you should be able to navigate the trail to Steuben even though at times it is sandy or periodically covered by water because of beaver activity. Between M-94 and Steuben, the trail crosses only one other road, contains 11 of the 14 bridges, and briefly borders the Big Island Lake Wilderness.

The section of the trail south of Steuben has been washed away by beavers and is temporarily closed. The best alternate is to take Thunderlake Road east 1.5 miles to M-94 and then south one mile to where the trail again crosses the highway. Not only will this bypass the temporary beaver damage, but it gets you past this section's

Beaver

These frumpy, nocturnal rodents are responsible for more than impassable, log-trodden, waterlogged trails. They had an incisive role in the history of the North American continent. Long before logs were commercially harvested, these enterprising little lumberjacks were felling trees, damming ponds and engineering sophisticated canal systems. That is, until beavers were harvested in great numbers.

From the early 1650s to the late 1850s, beaver pelt trading flourished. In fact, beaver was considered money, and millions of rodents were slaughtered until demand for the pelts waned in the mid-19th century.

An illustrious engineer, the beaver is superbly engineered. A flat, rudder-like tail propels it through water, yet acts as a brace for balance when gnawing at trees; its fat and thick fur (which the beaver waterproofs by smearing with a greasy discharge stored in oil glands) insulate like a wet suit; and valve-like ears and nose close off under water.

This ugly duckling that lumbers about on land turns into a sleek swan in the water. It creates wetlands by building dams

▶

An obvious sign of beavers' presence

Beaver, *cont.*

so that it can safely maneuver around to its favorite food sources: deciduous trees, saplings, shrubs and aquatic plants.

Since beavers are nocturnal, you are more likely to see the effects of beavers, rather than the actual animals. Orange enamel-coated incisors gnaw away at trees that, when felled, are towed and put into place to create dams. A rise in the water level upstream creates a pond. Branches, tree trunks, grasses, and mud are woven together into dome-like lodges as part of a family effort.

The ponds are a boon for other animals. Aquatic animals inhabit the ponds, where fish-eating birds often visit. And, moose, deer and elk (which thrive on aquatic vegetation) expand their range. Oh, and, impassable, log-trodden, waterlogged trails are an effective deterrent for humans.

deep sand. (For those users not impeded by sand, a shorter bypass takes you only 0.8 miles along Thunderlake Road to a an unimproved road that soon accesses the rail-trail. From here to the M-94 alternate link, the trail is very sandy.)

Once back on the grade past the second M-94 crossing, the trail becomes a hard-packed two-track that passes through a recently-logged area. About 1.5 miles from M-94, another trail veers off to the right, which will take you off the grade to Indian River Camp and Picnic Grounds a mile away. Continuing along the trail, don't worry about those "hippo backs" you see rising along the trail—they are merely large ant mounds.

Two additional problem areas occur 4.4 and 4.7 miles after the trail crosses M-94 for the third time. The first is in a large wet area where hunks of gravel fill in where the trail washed out. The second, near the Hiawatha Station, is a sandy stretch that will give some trail users problems.

Less than two miles after crossing State Route 94 for the fourth and last time, a two-track service drive intersects the trail. If you were to head west along it, this sandy unimproved road runs 0.8

miles to a snowmobile parking area off M-94 that could serve as a southern access point. This is 4.5 miles north of Manistique. The parking area is large enough to accommodate several horse trailers. A sign on the east side of M-94 denotes that this is the Haywire trail.

Proceeding along the rail-trail past the service drive, the trail is only about 4.5 miles from the southern trailhead next to the Manistique Water Intake Plant and Park, which is along the southern edge of the Indian River. About 3.7 miles past the service drive, a snowmobile trail takes a sharp left away from the corridor—don't be tempted to take this. Stay on the railgrade another 0.3 miles where an arrow points to the left. Turn left here and left again when the road forks soon thereafter. You are off the grade at this point. Continue for 0.1 mile and then turn right and follow a clearing that leads to the river. This is a short, sandy stretch.

The trail then reenters the trees on your right before veering left to cross the river, where a boardwalk has been constructed over the dam at the intake plant. The park here has a small picnic area with barbecue grills and parking.

To get to this southern trailhead, follow M-94 north from U.S. 2 at Manistique to Riverview (a road that traverses the south border of the Indian River) and turn east following the road to the parking area just beyond the water intake plant.

Kal-Haven Trail Sesquicentennial State Park

Endpoints: West of Kalamazoo to east of South Haven

Location: Kalamazoo and Van Buren Counties

Length: 34 miles

Surface: Crushed stone

Uses:

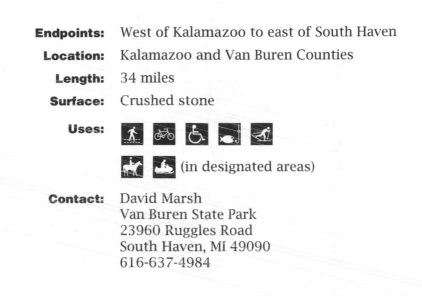 (in designated areas)

Contact: David Marsh
Van Buren State Park
23960 Ruggles Road
South Haven, MI 49090
616-637-4984

◆◆◆

I t may have seemed like it to trail proponents, but the Kal-Haven Trail didn't really take 150 years to complete. So why Sesquicentennial?

When the trail's Master Plan was developed, it looked like the trail would open in 1987, the same year the State of Michigan would celebrate its 150th anniversary, or Sesquicentennial. The rail corridor originated at the time of statehood, so it seemed logical to lengthen the trail's name in tribute. Ironically, the trail opened in 1989.

The eastern trailhead is located on 10th Street, west of the City of Kalamazoo and U.S. 131 and north of Michigan State Route 43. There is a refurbished caboose at the site, serving a new role as an office and information center. You also will find plenty of parking,

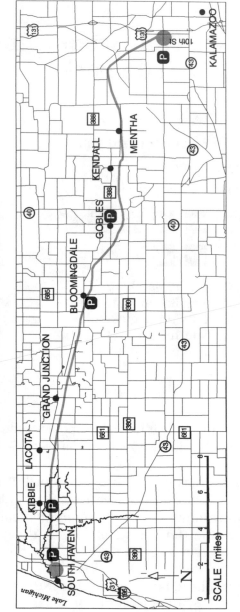

KAL-HAVEN TRAIL SESQUICENTENNIAL STATE PARK

Marg Peterson

Near Beehive Farm Market

pit toilets and water. During the summer, volunteers staff the caboose.

Start off along the trail by heading into the trees in a northerly direction. The trail slopes gradually downward as it heads toward Lake Michigan—keep this in mind for the return trip. Mile markers will help you gauge your trip, which begins in a wooded area and contains some steep slopes alongside the grade. After traveling about four miles, you will curve to the left and head in a more westerly direction for the rest of the route.

As the landscape changes to flat, open fields, you are approaching Mentha. Once known as the mint capital of the world, it now serves as a center for radish production. Beyond this town (about 10 miles into your trip), you will arrive at Bee Hive Farm Market, which is a good place to stop. In addition to a small grocery store, a bakery, petting farm, camping area and other surprises await you.

The next community is Gobles, which also offers several eateries. From here you are less then five miles to the midway point of the trail at the restored depot in Bloomingdale. Originally built for the Kalamazoo and South Haven Railroad in 1870, the depot is located on an acre of land donated by Augustus Haven (in the park named in his honor). Restored in 1987, the depot now serves as a museum, meeting place and rest stop—a haven for weary trail users.

Friends of the Kal-Haven Trail

Organized in 1984, the "Friends" have been instrumental to the growing success of the Kal-Haven Trail. First, working with the Michigan Department of Natural Resources, the Friends helped secure funding for acquisition and development of the trail from the Michigan Natural Resources Trust Fund. Today, the Friends work closely with the DNR Parks Division to help operate, manage and further develop the trail.

Using a unique partnership approach to park management, the trail was built as a state park and is jointly operated by the Friends and the DNR Parks Division. No tax dollars are used to operate the trail. The friends fund trail maintenance and operation through user fees, community and private donations as well as special fundraising events, such as the successful Trailblazer bike ride held every May.

From Bloomingdale to Grand Junction the trail is a little more than six miles. You are close when you cross the camelback bridge over Barber Creek, about a mile east of town. From Grand Junction, where refreshments are available, stopping places are limited. Lacota is about three miles away and near Kibbie, a family has opened a refreshment stand alongside the trail.

You will discover blueberry country near the end of the trail (July is the peak season). The trail's end is near when you cross the Black River on a covered bridge, which was constructed by the Michigan Civilian Conservation Corps in 1988 in memory of Donald F. Nichols. His family donated the materials.

The trail follows the Black River, under Interstate 196, to its temporary western terminus on Bluestar Highway, just south of the Black River. Limited parking, a picnic area and pit toilets are available. With the assistance of the Michigan Department of Transportation, the trail has been extended under the highway, along the river. In 1994, a new trailhead in South Haven should be completed.

Other new features for 1994 include the completion of a parallel equestrian trail from 68th street (two-miles west of South

Haven) all the way to Bloomingdale, as well as the construction of a pedestrian crossing over the active railroad tracks at Grand Junction.

Because this facility is a state park, you will need a user pass. These passes, which generate a major source of revenue for trail operations, can be purchased at various businesses in the communities along the route, as well as from park rangers and volunteers who patrol the trail or staff the caboose. Individual daily passes cost $2 and annual passes are $10. Family daily passes cost $5 and annual family passes are $25. Passes purchased on the Kal-Haven Trail are valid for use on other state park rail-trails.

A grand bridge over the Grand River along the Kent Trails

Kent Trails

Endpoints: John Ball Park in Grand Rapids to Byron Center

Location: Kent County

Length: 13 miles, 7.5 miles on an abandoned rail corridor.

Surface: Asphalt

Uses:

Contact: Roger Sabine, Assistant Director of Planning
Kent County Road and Park Commission
1500 Scribner, N.W.
Grand Rapids, MI 49504
616-242-6948

◆ ◆ ◆

Stitched through the fabric of the state's second largest metropolitan area, the Kent Trails system weaves together a resource that is both scenic and valuable. Resulting from the collaborative effort of six governmental entities, this system provides a unique opportunity for individuals and families to enjoy the outdoors close to home.

As the trail threads through the urban patchwork, it passes industrial sites, winds along and over the Grand River, runs beside and under Interstate 196 and meanders through the rural countryside. All of it tied together by the abandoned railroad, road corridors, surface streets and easements donated by private landowners to create the linear trail.

The northern end of the trail can be reached from John Ball Park, which offers a zoo and parking. Head south from the park (by

KENT TRAILS

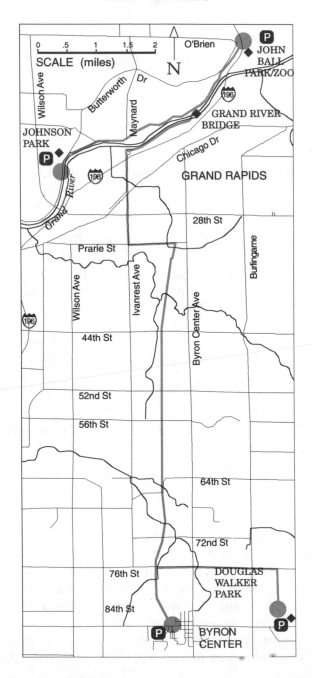

road) to the trailhead, which is across the street next to the Coca-Cola bottling plant, to begin your adventure.

After passing the bottling plant, the trail takes you to where trains once ran under the highway, then alongside the Interstate, behind an industrial building and into the trees. Suddenly you are surrounded by nature and traveling alongside the Grand River. The hum from the highway is the only sign that you are not in the wilderness.

Nearly two miles into the trail you will reach a junction. If you go straight, a spur trail will take you to Johnson Park in about three miles (this could also serve as an access point). The main trail turns left and crosses the Grand River on an old railroad bridge, which is one of the trail's highlights. To the right, an abandoned trestle stands out in the wilderness.

After crossing the bridge, the trail turns right and uses a tree-lined road along the Grand River for more than a mile. The trail then turns left, goes under the highway, and soon passes the City of Wyoming's water treatment plant. The corridor narrows as it passes by the plant, which has five-foot fencing on either side of the trail. Attached to the fence are six signs in the style of the old Burma Shave ads that invite cyclers to Tour de Sewer.

Past the plant, for the next 1.8 miles, use the road or sidewalk depending on your mode of transportation. The trail crosses an active railroad line and busy Chicago Drive, then continues south for almost a mile on Ivanrest. At Prairie Street the route turns left and then right onto the rail grade less than a mile later.

Shortly after crossing Buck Creek and passing through a wooded area, the trail cuts away from the corridor to bypass a condominium complex and an industrial park. At 44th Street, the route crosses at the light and immediately turns left and continues along a short stretch of sidewalk before turning right back to the old rail corridor.

The next 5.1 miles continue on the old Lakeshore & Michigan Southern Railway grade, originally constructed in 1869. This section of the trail passes through a mixture of youthful subdivisions, rural residential housing and farmland. At 76th Street, four miles into this section, a left turn takes you along a paved shoulder for about two miles to a trail into Douglas Walker Park, where parking is available.

Continuing across 76th Street down the final mile of the grade, go under the pedestrian bridges at the golf course and meander in to Byron Center, where you will find several restaurants. The big white chicken at the Byron Center Motel signals your arrival. Limited parking is available where the trail ends on 84th Street.

Kiwanis Trail

Endpoints: Maumee Road west of downtown Adrian to West Valley Road in the City of Adrian

Location: Lenawee County

Length: 3.4 miles

Surface: Asphalt

Uses:

Contact: Mark Gasche, Community Service Director
Adrian City Hall
100 East Church Street
Adrian, MI 49221
517-263-2161

❖ ❖ ❖

Trestle Park, near the Kiwanis Trail's southern end puts this trail in a league of its own. Of all the facilities developed along a rail-trail, this may be the finest. The City of Adrian truly did itself proud, but trying to describe Trestle Park is almost a disservice—you need to see it to really get a feel for what has been created.

Located at the old trestle on the South Branch of the River Raisin, the park uses a turn-of-the century railroad-style motif on the built structures, which include two picnic shelters, an amphitheater and restrooms. The park also features a baseball diamond, a pedestrian bridge over the river, lighted pathways (other than the rail-trail), parking and—of course—the trestle. Parking is located on Hunt Street off M-52 just north of downtown.

Oh, and the trail is nice too!

KIWANIS TRAIL

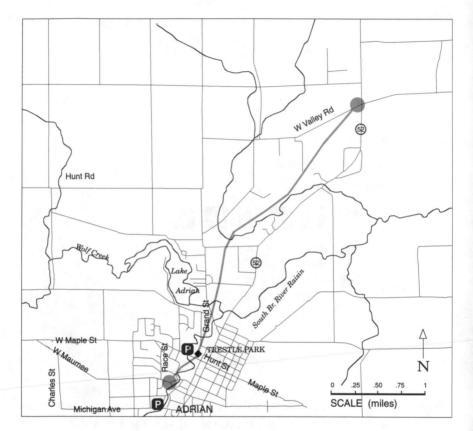

The southern trailhead is located along the parking lot for the Country Market/Arbor Drugs complex off Maumee Road west of downtown, almost a half-mile south of Trestle Park. The trail here is narrow, and at the northeast end of the parking lot, the trail makes a jog around a fenced-in area by using local roads. After passing through an old industrial area, the trail crosses the South Branch of the River Raisin and Maple Avenue before entering Trestle Park.

Beyond Trestle Park, and shortly after crossing Bent Oak Avenue, the trail comes to a long bridge over Wolf Creek. The next 2.3

Trestle Park

On an early summer day in 1992, more than 1,500 people turned out to witness the unveiling of a dream—Trestle Park. Spearheaded by Adrian Community Services Director Ray Maxe, this was the culmination of a 20-year effort.

Recognized as the largest single development ever undertaken by the City of Adrian, the project stitched together 10 separate pieces of property. With its bridges over the river, trails, amphitheater, baseball diamond (funded by General Telephone), pavilions and restrooms, the park cost more than $1.7 million to develop. The project was funded, without any taxpayers' money, through the Harriet Kimball Fee Trust Fund, which had been bequeathed to the city for beautification projects.

In its first year of operation, the park received awards from the Michigan Chapter of the American Society of Landscape Architects and the International Society of Horticulture.

Trestle Park

miles are quite scenic, passing through a rolling landscape with a mix of residences, farm fields and woods. The trail crosses Beaver Creek and parallels a wooded ravine. No parking exists at the trail's north end, but plans call for the trail to extend north toward Tecumseh.

LakeLands Trail State Park

Endpoints: Stockbridge to Pinckney

Location: Ingham and Livingston Counties

Length: 12 miles, will be 36 miles when completed

Surface: Crushed stone

Uses:

Contact: Jon LaBossiere
Pinckney Recreation Area
8555 Silver Hill, Route 1
Pinckney, MI 48169
313-426-4913

◆ ◆ ◆

f it's true that good things come to those that wait, then this trail is really great news. The LakeLands Trail State Park officially opens in 1994—at least the first 12 miles. More waiting is required for the other 24 miles.

The trail resulted from a unique arrangement between the Michigan Departments of Transportation and Natural Resources. Abandoned in 1975, the corridor was purchased by MDOT two years later. The two departments agreed that MDOT would acquire and retain title to the corridor and DNR would operate and maintain the completed facility as a state park. To make a long story short, years of inactivity finally ended when trail surfacing commenced between Stockbridge and Pinckney in October of 1993.

The newest of the three state park rail-trails, the LakeLand's attractive rural setting and proximity to major population centers could combine to make this one of Michigan's most popular rail-trails.

LAKELANDS TRAIL STATE PARK

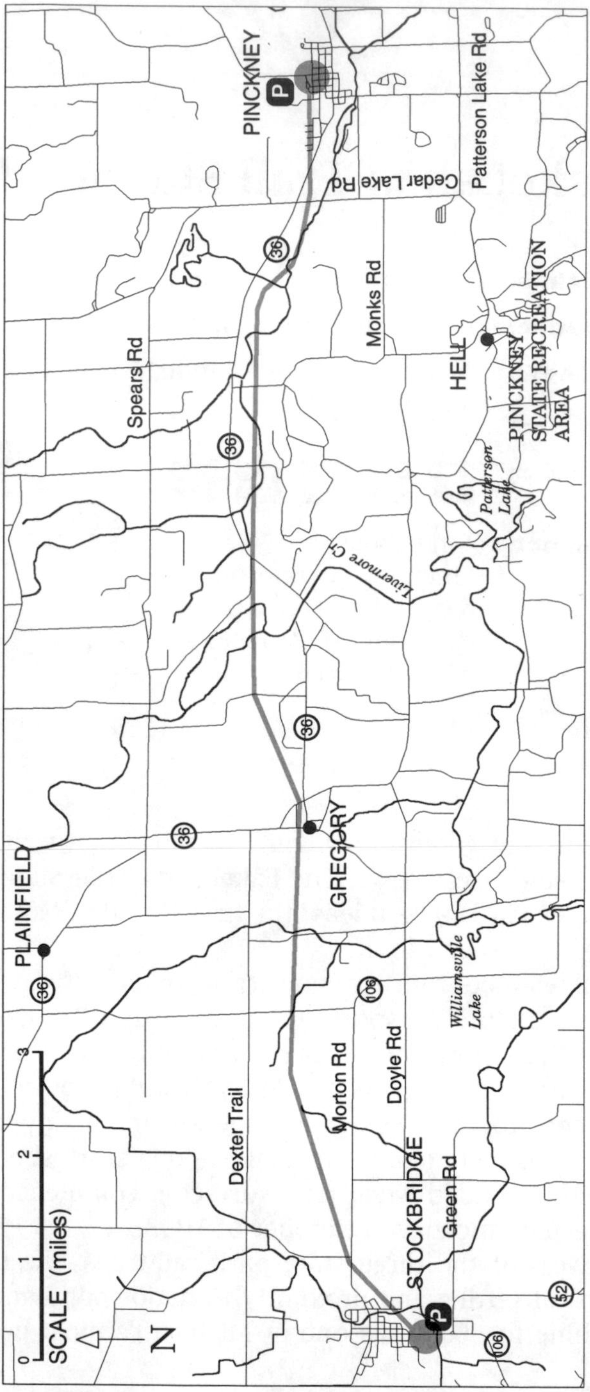
PINCKNEY
P
Patterson Lake Rd
Cedar Lake Rd
36
Monks Rd
Spears Rd
HELL
PINCKNEY
STATE RECREATION
AREA
Patterson
Lake
Livermore Cr
GREGORY
PLAINFIELD
106
Williamsville
Lake
Morton Rd
Doyle Rd
Dexter Trail
STOCKBRIDGE
Green Rd
52
SCALE (miles)
0
1
2
3
N

At Stockbridge (the temporary western trailhead), parking is available at the park-and-ride lot on M-52/106, south of the historic Stockbridge Township Hall on the village square. The trail heads northeast past the village and soon veers to the right toward the community of Gregory some five miles away. Because the corridor was abandoned nearly 20 years ago, the mature vegetation provides a pleasant setting for the trail user.

The LakeLands Trail offers an excellent setting for a nature hike.

Stop in Gregory for refreshments before completing the next seven miles to Pinckney. At Pinckney (the temporary eastern trailhead), parking is available at the old Pinckney depot—the last remaining railroad building on the trail. The depot is located on Pinckney Road, northeast of the downtown area.

In 1994, additional trail surfacing is scheduled for completion between Pinckney and the Village of Hamburg, about seven miles away. When fully completed, the trail will stretch 29 miles from northeast of Jackson to the Village of Hamburg. A seven-mile eastern section also will be developed from South Lyon, which is completing its own two-mile rail-trail in 1994, to the City of Wixom.

Little Falls Trail

Endpoints: Buck Lake Road, 3.0 miles east of Watersmeet to Little Falls, 1.2 miles north of USFS Road 172

Location: Gogebic and Ontonagon Counties

Length: 6.5 miles (although the trail is seasonally open to a larger network snowmobiling trails); 5.5 miles on an abandoned rail corridor

Surface: Dirt, gravel, sand, cinders, old trees and washout

Uses:

Contact: Wayne Petterson, District Ranger
U.S. Forest Service
P. O. Box 276
Watersmeet, MI 49969
906-358-4551

◆◆◆

The surface of this trail is as tough as the surrounding landscape is peaceful. A provocative trail, it offers the explorer a sense of the deep forest experience.

To start this experience, take Buck Lake Road about 0.3 miles north of Old U.S. 2 (about three miles east of Watersmeet). You will see snowmobile signs to the right at the trail's beginning. Unfortunately, there is no parking nearby, so you'll have to park in Watersmeet (see Watersmeet/Land O' Lakes Trail on page 117).

The multi-use trail currently is only 6.5 miles long (the endpoint is currently to Little Falls), so you will likely loop back to your starting point. Plan on a 13-mile trek along the trail as well as the three

LITTLE FALLS TRAIL

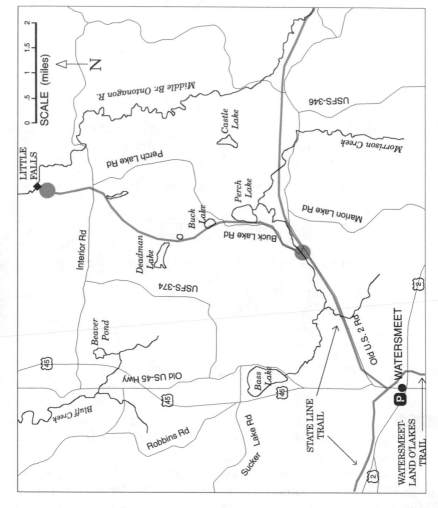

miles to and from your parking spot. The expedition is well worth it.

You will begin by winding through the woods on a rough trail that could stop you short in sand. Within a half-mile, you will actually get to the grade. Old ties, roots and pockets of sand make for one bumpy excursion!

Continue through the birch and aspen and in a mile you will approach Perch Lake, where you might be tempted to camp. This is the Ottawa National Forest, so you can camp without a permit, but use proper etiquette: do not cut down any live trees or plants; put out campfires before leaving the campsite; and pack out any trash.

Back on the trail, you will not have made it past the lake when you start tiptoeing through the effects of beaver—dams, felled trees and water over the trail. In less than a mile you will reach Buck Lake.

More than half a mile beyond the lake, the trail forks. Bear to the left even though the trail seems more worn to the right. A tree displays a sign for the trail, but you can barely see it. In another quarter-mile, you will reach a land bridge through a scenic stretch before a maze of old railroad ties leads you into a canopy of trees. Put on your waders   you are in for another wet stretch until you reach

Along the shore at Perch Lake

a dirt road, Forest Highway 172 (Interior Road). At this point you could double back by turning right here, then right again on Forest Highway 171.

If you are more ambitious, continue nearly 1.5 miles to Little Falls, which are definitively little. Keep in mind that this section is very rough—beaver and human logging activities have impacted the route. Stop and enjoy the falls before turning back (private ownership interweaves thereafter, so turn back). From Forest Highway 172 you can either come back on the trail or take the alternate route along Forest Highway 171, which eventually brings you back to Old U.S. 2.

Little Traverse Wheelway

Endpoints: Bayfront Park to west of Bay View Village in the City of Petoskey

Location: Emmet County

Length: 1 mile (at Bayfront Park) of a 2.25 mile trail is on an abandoned rail corridor.

Surface: Asphalt

Uses:

Contact: Brad Leech, City Planner
100 West Lake Street
Petoskey, MI 49770
616-347-2500

◆ ◆ ◆

Bayfront Park provides the picturesque setting for the Little Traverse Wheelway. Here, along Little Traverse Bay, the trail lies nestled between the waters of Lake Michigan and the bluff upon which the City of Petoskey is located.

The entire Wheelway is 2.25 miles long. From the west city limits to Bayfront Park, the route uses roads and sidewalks and passes through Magnus and Mineral Wells Parks. The section of the wheelway on the abandoned rail corridor is at Bayfront Park.

The trail starts behind the Little Traverse Historical Society History Museum, which is housed in the old Chicago and West Michigan Railway Station. There is limited parking at the museum, but parking can be found elsewhere in the park. The asphalt soon passes a pedestrian tunnel under U.S. 31, providing safe access to and from downtown. The trail also passes a marina, a softball field and a

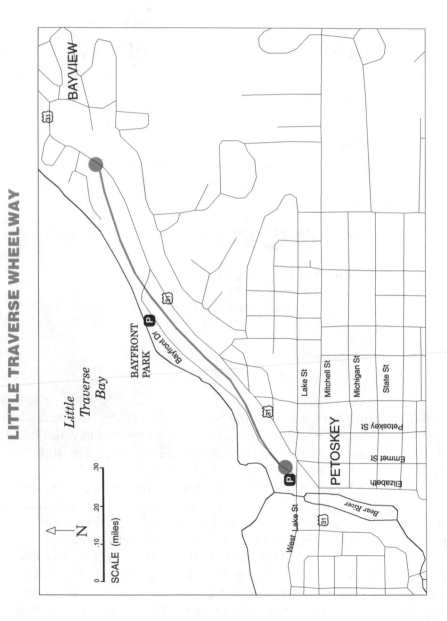

resource center, which offers a children's play area, public restrooms and drinking fountains. A brick walkway with ornate lighting leads to the bay.

Midway along the trail, a picnic area is provided near a little waterfall off the bluff and a wooden stairway provides access to a small park on top of the bluff. From this vantage point, you can see a spectacular view of Little Traverse Bay.

The trail continues past a small pond, and eventually runs behind a commercial area on U.S. 31. The Wheelway uses a paved sidewalk at U.S. 31 to continue into the historic resort community of Bay View.

While the Little Traverse Wheelway currently serves primarily local needs, its role in the future will broaden. It has already been designated as a part of the route for the North Country National Scenic Trail. And, as other area trail projects are completed, it will become a key piece in a trail system that stretches across the "tip of the mitt."

Overlooking the trail and Little Traverse Bay

A mile marker near Mackinaw City reminds users of the trail's heritage.

Mackinaw/Alanson Trail

Endpoints: Mackinaw City to Alanson

Location: Emmet County

Length: 24 miles

Surface: Dirt, gravel, sand and original ballast

Uses:

Contact: Duane Hoffman
District Fire and Recreation Specialist
Mackinaw State Forest
P.O. Box 660
Gaylord, MI 49735
517-732-3541

❖❖❖

Recognizing that opportunities exist to combine recreation with other forms of economic development, the Michigan Bell Telephone Company donated this corridor to the Michigan Department of Natural Resources in the late 1980s. Abandoned railroad corridors are ideal for the placement of high-technology underground fiber-optic cables and Michigan Bell buried cable along this route, which now exists in harmony with the surface trail use.

Completed in 1882 by the Grand Rapids and Indiana Railroad, this was the second railroad line to reach the Straits of Mackinac, one year after the Michigan Central Railroad had attained the same goal. Abandoned in 1982, by 1989 it had become the corridor that linked together the Upper and Lower Peninsulas for snowmobiling. The Mackinac Bridge Authority agreed to transport riders and their machines across the bridge for a small fee, a service that already existed for bicyclists.

MACKINAW/ALANSON TRAIL

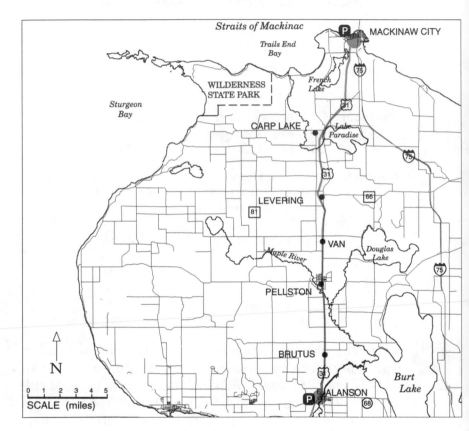

The trail begins in Mackinaw City, west of Interstate 75, behind the Chalet House Motel and Shepler's Ferry parking lot. Carol Wilson, owner of the Chalet House Motel, has indicated that people using the trail may park in her lot as long as they check with her at the front desk.

Looking like a narrow country road, the trail starts by sweeping left through progressively-larger trees for less than a mile. Then, shortly after straightening, the trail makes its first road crossing at Trails End Road. If you go right, a 1.5-mile side-trip will take you to Trail's End Bay on Lake Michigan.

The next 5.7 miles are among the most enjoyable of the whole trail. Cutting across a large portion of state forest property, the trail is interrupted only twice by road crossings, though it does parallel U.S. 31 for a few miles north of Carp Lake. Within this section, the North Country National Scenic Trail merges with the corridor from Wilderness State Park.

At Gill Road, the Carp Lake General Store is a convenient place to stop, and you will see Lake Paradise on your left. South of Carp Lake, U.S. 31 veers away from the trail and from here to south of Levering, the trail is enjoyable and again passes through state forest property. At Levering, the community has cut a path from the trail to its business district on U.S. 31.

South of Levering the trail veers toward U.S. 31 where it remains for much of the distance to Alanson. This section has not gotten the use that the northern portion has and can be a very rough ride. For the less adventurous, it may be advisable to use Levering as an endpoint for this trail until improvements are made to the southern part of the trail.

For the diehard rail-trail rider, the trip has just begun, although the trail's proximity to the road make it easy to stop at a store or gas station or to opt for on-road travel if the trail proves troublesome.

You will find two deviations from the corridor in the Pellston area, the first occurs north of town at the airport. At Ely Road turn left and then right on to the shoulder of U.S. 31. Use the shoulder until south of the airport entrance where it is possible to access the corridor from a driveway. The second is in town, where it is necessary to use local streets to bypass the old depot.

After crossing Maple River south of Pellston, the trail is a straight shot until north of Alanson. Here the trail veers away from U.S. 31 behind a residential area. The trail cuts through several hills along this stretch, before ending at the foot of the Hillside Gardens in Alanson. Parking is available at a park-and-ride lot just north of the trailhead on U.S. 31.

The old R.G. Peters Grade, which is now part of the Nordhouse Dunes Trail System

Nordhouse Dunes Trail System

Endpoints: Southern boundary of the Nordhouse Dunes
Wilderness Area to the Lake Michigan
Recreation Area in Manistee National Forest

Location: Mason County

Length: 2.5 miles

Surface: Sand

Uses:

Contact: Greg Peterson, Forester
USDA Forest Service
1658 Manistee Highway
Manistee, MI 49660
616-723-2211

◆◆◆

The only federally-designated wilderness in the Lower Peninsula, Nordhouse Dunes Wilderness Area provides a unique opportunity to get away from the hustle and bustle of everyday life. Located along Lake Michigan, this area encompasses 3,450 acres. Most of the dunes are 3,500 to 4,000 years old and some are as high as 140 feet. Unlike other dune systems, this one is interspersed with woody vegetation.

While the trails that traverse the dunes can be physically challenging, the old R.G. Peters logging railroad grade offers the opportunity for a less strenuous wilderness experience. You can access the trail from the south off Nurnberg Road. A small parking area is located on the north side of the road six miles west of Quarterline Road. Be forewarned: neither the parking area nor trail is marked.

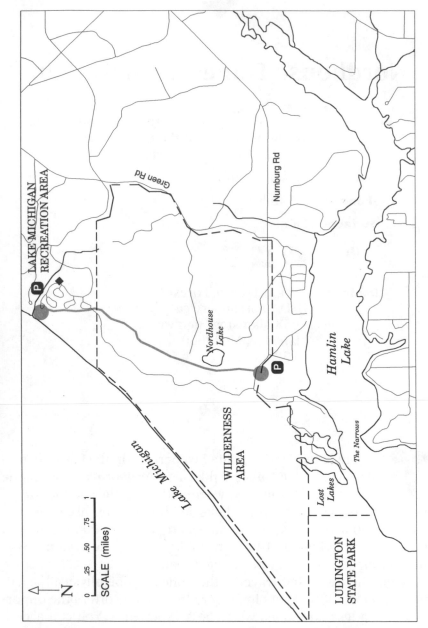

NORDHOUSE DUNES TRAIL SYSTEM

LAKE MICHIGAN
RECREATION AREA

Green Rd

Numburg Rd

Nordhouse
Lake

Hamlin
Lake

Lake Michigan

WILDERNESS
AREA

The Narrows

Lost
Lakes

LUDINGTON
STATE PARK

SCALE (miles)

0   .25   .50   .75   1

N

The first part of the trail heads north through a mixture of beech, maple, oak and pine. The trail is easy to follow until it reaches Nordhouse Lake, where the best option is to follow around on the west side of the lake until you pick up the grade on the north. Do not go up the embankment unless you want to end up on a different trail. Stay close to the lake.

North of the lake, the trail meanders through forest while periodically dipping into more swampy surroundings—insect repellent is a must. A tree-lined dune will be your companion on the left.

After passing through marsh grass, the trail leaves the wilderness area and enters the Lake Michigan Recreation Area. Here, the trail surface is packed gravel and is part of a bicycle trail through the woods. The trail continues past a camping area and several interpretive plaques before arriving at the southern observation platform in the recreation area. Here you can access Lake Michigan and other trails. Parking is available for those who would like to start from the recreation area.

You can spend the night in the Wilderness Area with a few limitations: no campsites or campfires are allowed within 400 feet of Lake Michigan and Wilderness boundaries, or within 200 feet of Nordhouse Lake; No group camping (more than 10 people); bring your own water and pack out your trash. Finally, no public nudity is allowed.

Less primitive camping is available at the Lake Michigan Recreation Area, which features 100 campsites, as well as toilets, hand pumps for water, fire rings and picnic tables. Open year-round and managed from mid-May to mid-September, the area offers no showers or electricity. There is a fee to use the campsites, and advance reservations are possible for an additional fee by calling the Mistics Corporation at 1-800-283-2267.

Shawn Richardson

Entrepreneurs make the most of the Paint Creek Trail.

Paint Creek Trail

Endpoints: Rochester to Lake Orion

Location: Oakland County

Length: Currently 8.5 miles, will be 10.5 miles when completed

Surface: Crushed stone

Uses:

![horse] in designated areas only

Contact: Linda Gorecki, Trailways Coordinator
Paint Creek Trailways Commission
4393 Collins Road
Rochester, MI 48064
313-651-9260

◆◆◆

The huffing and puffing of breathless bicyclists, walkers and joggers along Paint Creek has replaced the chugging sound of trains that once labored to rise the 300-foot incline from the Clinton River to Lake Orion.

Originally constructed by the short-lived Detroit and Bay City Railroad in the 1860s, the corridor served passengers and the region's bean growers successively as the Michigan Central Railroad, the New York Central and finally the ill-fated Penn Central until its bankruptcy in 1976. Now the corridor serves as an excellent non-motorized route only 20 miles north of Detroit.

Among the delights of this trail are peaceful scenery, glacial rock formations, two rivers, eight miles of trout fishing, cider mills and nearly a dozen bridges.

PAINT CREEK TRAIL

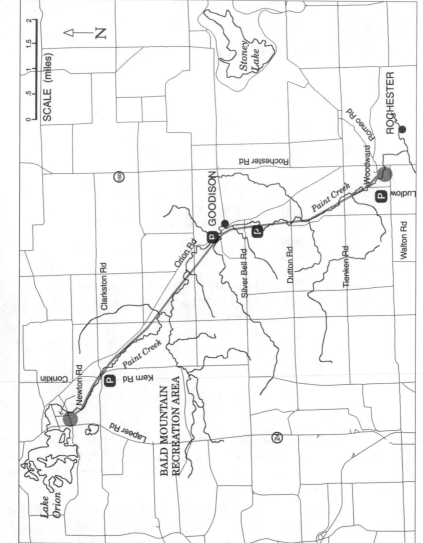

For simplicity, the trail starts at the City of Rochester's Municipal Park. Parking is located off Ludlow Road on the west side of the park. You will find the trail on the northern edge of the park using the park's internal trail system. Be sure to turn left on the trail—a right turn will take you downtown.

After crossing Ludlow, the trail will quickly cross the creek and arrive at a trail leading into the Dinosaur Hill Nature Preserve. The preserve includes several self-guided trails, a picnic area and an interpretive center.

The first major road crossing after leaving the preserve is Tienken Road. Use caution crossing this busy road, where parking is available on the north side. You will find a walkway down to the water shortly after crossing the creek a second time.

For the next couple of miles you may notice that the creek's banks have been reinforced with logs or rocks. This is the work of Clinton Valley Trout Unlimited. Paint Creek is the major remaining trout stream in the Detroit metropolitan area and the rocks and logs were placed to stabilize eroding portions of the creek, which were making the water too silty for the trout's liking.

North of Silver Bell Road (where there is a small parking lot), a larger set of steps provides access to the water at a scenic curve in the creek. This is your signal that you will soon arrive at the Paint Creek Cider Mill—a favorite destination of trail users seeking cider,

One of the many bridges over Paint Creek

donuts and other delectables. Parking is provided along the trail north of Gallagher Road.

In addition to its many scenic bridge crossings, the Paint Creek Trail has relatively few major road crossings for an urban area. The next 3.7 miles are no exception; the trail only crosses two roads before reaching the parking area at Kern Road. You are now in the Bald Mountain State Recreation Area, which includes cedar swamps, bogs and scenic vistas. In addition, the Trout and Lower Trout Lakes offer swimming, boating and fishing.

In this same stretch of trail, you will pass through the Royal Oak Archery Club, which should add some excitement to your journey. Also, you may be fortunate enough to view an eclectic collection of llama, elk, sheep and peacocks that reside on an adjacent landowners' property.

The last section of the trail is somewhat anti-climactic. While you do pass the largest pond along the route, the trail just (sort of) ends at Newton Road on the edge of Lake Orion. For the adventuresome (and the hungry), the corridor does continue into Lake Orion. The corridor ends at a supermarket parking lot that just happens to be near an ice cream parlor.

Pere Marquette Rail-Trail of Mid-Michigan

Endpoints: City of Midland

Location: Midland County

Length: 3 miles, will be 30 miles when completed

Surface: Asphalt

Uses:

Contact: Bill Gibson, Director
Midland County Parks and Recreation
Department
220 West Ellsworth Street
Midland, MI 48640-5194
517-832-6870

◆◆◆

Thd Pere Marquette is Michigan's version of a rail-trail Lamborghini. Its detailed planning, distinctive styling and quality handiwork garner quite a bit of well-deserved attention. But, what really puts this trail out in front of the pack is its speed: The city section went from zero to three miles in four years, and the county portion is projected to go from zero to 11.6 miles in five years, dating from the time of abandonment.

The driver behind the rail-trail has been the Midland Foundation, which purchased the corridor from Midland to Clare and retained ownership within the Midland city limits. It was this three-mile section that was completed in 1993. The foundation gave the remainder of the corridor to the Midland County Parks and Recreation Commission.

PERE MARQUETTE RAIL-TRAIL OF MID-MICHIGAN

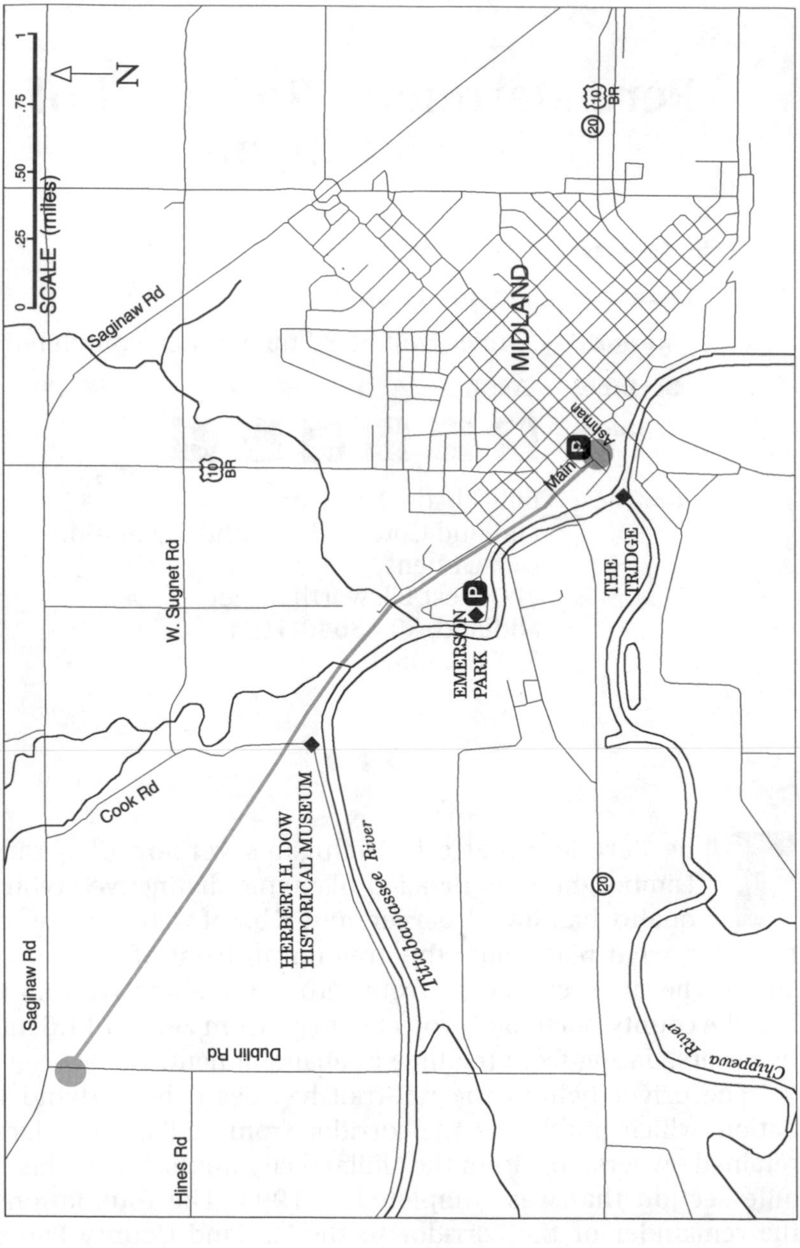

SCALE (miles)
0   .25   .50   .75   1

N

Saginaw Rd

10
BR

W. Sugnet Rd

Cook Rd

Saginaw Rd

Hines Rd

Dublin Rd

HERBERT H. DOW
HISTORICAL MUSEUM

Tittabawassee River

EMERSON
PARK

P

MIDLAND

Main St

Ashman

P

THE
TRIDGE

20

Chippewa River

20
BR

10
BR

The trail begins near the "tridge" (a bridge with three segments) at the confluence of the Tittabawassee and Chippewa Rivers and the Farmers Market at the end of Ashman Road. You will find parking and restrooms here. The trail heads northwest from this point, paralleling the Tittabawassee River for 1.3 miles.

Two rail-trail enthusiasts enjoy the trail along the Tittabawassee River.

The first half-mile takes you under M-20, past two fishing decks built along the river, through a residential area and past Hart Park with its gazebo and benches overlooking the river and trail. At the first road crossing, you will see a sign on the left for the historic Upper Bridge and, after crossing, an entrance to Emerson Park.

When you reach the old cement mile marker (SAG 21), you are 21 miles from Saginaw and you have traveled one mile on the trail. The bridge you soon cross has the name of the rail-trail painted on the side in large letters. Then, just after the Tittabawassee River swings away to the left, the trail comes alongside the Herbert H. Dow Historical Museum.

The Cook Road crossing, currently the trail's halfway point, is the last road crossing until you reach the trail's end at Dublin Road. This section of trail is away from the hustle and bustle of the city, yet still provides access to the Northwood Institute and Dow High School. Near the SAG 22 marker is a wooden platform with benches overlooking a wetland.

An interesting feature of this trail are the barricades that keep motorized vehicles off while doubling as signs. Each barricade has a map of the trail (showing your location), the name of the street crossing and the number of miles to the next crossing.

In 1994, the county portion of the trail from Dublin Road to the community of North Bradley is scheduled for completion, adding an additional 11.6 miles to the existing trail. The new section will be 14 feet wide, an increase from the 12-feet-wide city section.

No matter what your mode of travel, this trail definitely warrants a test ride.

Republic/Champion Grade Trail

Endpoints: Champion to Bruce Creek Bridge, south of County Road 601

Location: Marquette County

Length: 7.5 miles

Surface: Dirt, gravel, sand and original ballast

Uses:

Contact: Dennis Nezich, Area Forest Manager
Ishpeming Forest Area
Escanaba River Station Forest
1985 U.S. 41 Highway West
Ishpeming, MI 49849
906-485-1031

◆◆◆

I t's no wonder that when the Department of Natural Resources decided to reintroduce moose into Michigan's Upper Peninsula, they chose to do so near the Van Riper State Park. Moose love aquatic vegetation, and this area certainly is aquatic. If one word can describe the general terrain that envelops the Republic/ Champion Grade Trail, it is WET.

Over its 7.5 mile course, the trail crosses 11 small bridges, skirts a couple of lakes and ponds, passes by bogs and beaver huts, and flows by and across creeks and rivers. Stop and enjoy the open water with grasses, cattails and water lilies. Watch the turtles sunning themselves and listen to the ducks splashing in the water.

Although the trail starts behind the mini-mart at Champion, there is no formal parking. Your best bet is to start at the Van Riper State

REPUBLIC/CHAMPION GRADE TRAIL

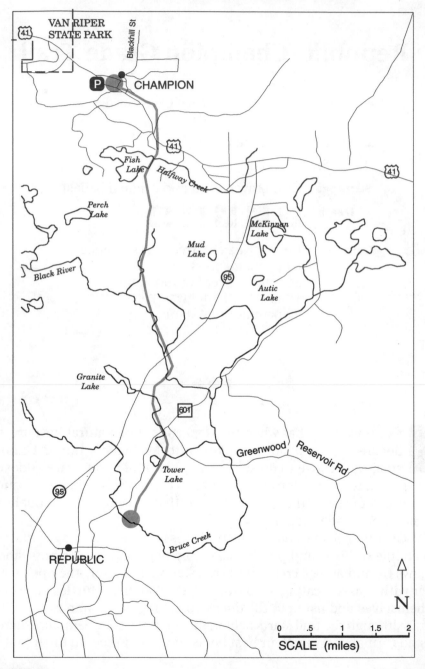

VAN RIPER
STATE PARK

Blackhill St

41

P   CHAMPION

41

41

Fish
Lake

Halfway Creek

Perch
Lake

McKinnon
Lake

Black River

Mud
Lake

95

Autic
Lake

Granite
Lake

601

Greenwood   Reservoir Rd

Tower
Lake

95

Bruce Creek

REPUBLIC

N

| 0 | .5 | 1 | 1.5 | 2 |
SCALE (miles)

Scenic view of wetlands near Fish Lake

Park and travel just more than a mile east along M-42/28 to the trailhead.

The first section of the trail (which parallels an active rail line) is wet and rutty until the angled crossing at M-42/28. The trail is firmer once you cross, and you will be on your way to a wetter wonderland—this time alongside the corridor, not in it. Once in a while you will get a break from the wet environment and cut through rock escarpments and past glacial rocks known as erratics. About 3.5 miles after the M-42/28 crossing you will cross M-95, which requires extra caution.

Moose

Moose droppings were once commonplace in the rich forests of Michigan's Upper Peninsula, until logging in the mid-1880s destroyed the moose's habitat and devastated its population.

To rectify the devastation, moose droppings took on new meaning in 1985 and 1987 when moose were lifted by helicopters from the Algonquin Provincial Park in Ontario, Canada and transported to Lake Michigamme, Michigan, where they were dropped off and released. These so-called "moose lifts" reintroduced 29 moose in 1985 and 30 moose in 1987—all northwest of Van Riper State Park.

This general area is again a suitable habitat for moose, who browse for twigs, leaves and bark of woody vegetation. Their favorite summer foods are the aquatic plants of marshes and wetlands, which are abundant in this area.

A species of the deer family, moose is the largest antlered animal in the world. Solitary animals, they mate in September or October, then cows give birth to 30-pound single or twin calves eight months later. Calves stay with their mothers for a year, until just before their siblings are born. Typical life-expectancy is about 20 years.

As of the summer of 1993, the product of the lifts resulted in an estimated population of 266 moose. The Department of Natural Resources' goal is to maintain a winter population of 1,000 moose by the year 2000. Hopefully, moose droppings will once again be ordinary.

For a more insightful overview on the Moose Lifts, visit the Van Riper State Park, where a kiosk offers excellent information.

David Kenyon

Look around and you might notice some fire scars as you approach a large bog. A short trek thereafter, the trail gets a little muddier (you might catch a glimpse of a beaver hut), then you get to County Road 601 about 1.5 miles after the 95 crossing.

If you want to go to Republic, you need to do so via 601: public ownership of the trail ends in 1.6 miles. To get to town, turn right on 601 and take the hilly, narrow road about 2.5 miles to the first stop and turn right into downtown. At your next stop, take a right again and go the short distance to the park in town, which has a small lake, picnic area and parking.

For those who wish to continue along the trail to its terminus, keep going the 1.6 miles once you cross County Road 601 to the second bridge along this small section. Public ownership of the trail ends here, so you'll have to turn around and either head back along the trail or take 601 into Republic.

State Line Trail

Endpoints: East of downtown Wakefield and
the Michigan/Wisconsin border south of
Mastedon Township Park

Location: Gogebic and Iron Counties

Length: 92.8 of a 102.2-mile trail are on an abandoned
rail corridor

Surface: Dirt, gravel, sand and original ballast;
wood chips in Iron River

Uses: 🚶 🚲 🐎 🛷

🛺 (in designated areas only)

Contacts: Jerry Divine
Area Forest Manager
Copper Country State Forest
1420 U.S. 2 West
Crystal Falls, MI 49920
906 875 6622

◆◆◆

Traversing both Gogebic and Iron Counties, this is Michigan's longest (and reddest) rail-trail. The discovery of iron (the county's namesake and the reason for the trail's color) spurred growth in the area in the mid-1800s. The Chicago and Northwestern Railroad followed suit in 1882 to ship out the stockpiled ore in the mines, and a future rail-trail was born. Abandoned in the early 1980s, the grade was purchased by the federal government in 1984.

This rugged trail can be negotiated with a mountain bike, but be warned that some sections of the trail become rough and rutty,

STATE LINE TRAIL

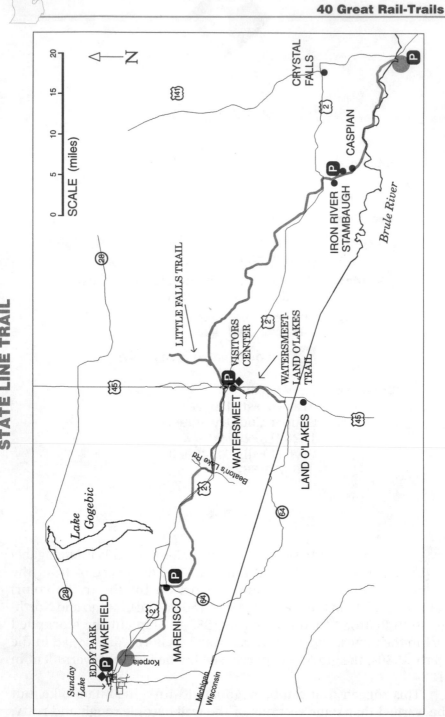

especially when the trail passes through actively (or recently) logged areas. Users will be placated by the trail's other magnificent features: forests of aspen, birch, maple, beech and hemlock; more than 50 bridges, often with incredible vistas over rivers; possible eagle sightings (Iron County is the Bald Eagle Capital of the Midwest); osprey nesting areas, particularly between Iron River and Stager; as well as old mines, lakes and farmland.

Stretching more than 100 miles and cutting through seven communities, the trail can more readily be understood if discussed in four sections.

Wakefield to Marenisco

Although the trail starts outside of Wakefield at Korpela Road less than a half-mile south of U.S. 2, getting there and finding parking (especially if you want to park overnight and enjoy the entire trail) will be a bit cumbersome. Getting to the trail from Wakefield can add more than five miles to the 11.2 mile Wakefield/Marenisco section of the trail. Parking is available at the Park-and-Ride lot at

Beautiful Barb Lake

U.S. 2 and Lake Shore Drive or at the Eddy Park Campground on
Sunday Lake. Day users could park along Korpela Road by the
trailhead.

Heading east from Korpela, the corridor starts out lined with
low, brushy vegetation and wildflowers before advancing into
smaller, then more stately, pines. After about two miles the trail
becomes more gravelly for a short section. Recent lumbering most
likely contributes to trail's poor condition. After the first dirt road
crossing about 3.5 miles into the trail, the corridor becomes a two-
track, but you will be rewarded with a beaver hut off to the right
within about three miles.

You will cross a second dirt road, and at the third the trail deviates from the rail corridor. Turn left on the dirt road and right at
the next one. Continue along this road past one road, and turn right
along the second one, which will get you back to the rail-trail. After
four small bridges (bicyclists should walk), a mix of meadowsweet
and goldenrod and a few stands of birch and aspen, you will arrive
at downtown Marenisco. Food and gas are available, as is parking at
the park near the pavilion.

Marenisco to Watersmeet

Since parking is available in Marenisco, you may want to start
here and travel the 33.2 miles (almost 24 are on the old rail line) to
Watersmeet. Shortly after passing behind the small commercial
and industrial section of Marenisco, a river begins to flow with the
trail. It crisscrosses the route several times, requiring you to cross
several bridges.

About 9.5 miles into this stretch, pick a few blackberries (season permitting) and take a break along Barb Lake, which is nestled
in the hills to the south. Once you start back along the trail, enjoy
the network of cattails before you get to the wet area caused by a
beaver dam. The next seven miles of the trail at times seem like a
dried-up stream bed, meandering over another eight bridges before
crossing under U.S. 2. From that point, you will travel another 3.4
miles on the trail (20 miles from Marenisco) before it deviates from
the corridor.

The re-route starts at Beatons Lake Road, which is a lightly-
traveled, two-lane road with no shoulder. Turn right and follow it

about 1.5 miles to Old U.S. 2 (you'll notice Roger's Bar). Take a left here and stay on the road for about seven miles. On the left, start looking for a trail marked "Trail #2 East". Turn left and take this bumpy, windy path a half-mile back up to the rail grade. Swing to the right and continue along the trail. (If you want to avoid this challenging half mile, stay on Old U.S. 2 for about another mile, then turn left up the dirt road to get to the corridor.)

Within about 2.5 miles, you will cross a bridge to get to a road with a canoe rental. If you don't care to take a paddling break, keep going past the railroad-tie graveyard until a fork in the trail. Stay to the left at the fork and Watersmeet is within a half-mile at Michigan State Route 45. Look to the right along M-45 and you will see the Watersmeet/Land O' Lakes Trail, an 8.8 mile trail that you can take as a diversion (see page 117).

Watersmeet to Iron River

If you continue on the State Line Trail, you will likely enjoy splendid isolation along the 36.6 mile journey to Iron River. Parking is available at the Watersmeet Visitor's Center or at the pavilion in town where the railroad roundhouse once existed.

Log stockpile near Iron River

Few people use the trail, which cuts through rock escarpment, sneaks past the Ottawa National Forest Watersmeet Ranger Station, crosses a few substantial bridges, teeters along land bridges, runs near meandering rivers and past beaver ponds, pounds through several sandy stretches and zips through the tiny community of Beechwood. You finally reach civilization again at Iron River—you know you're close when you see wood chips along the trail. Continue until U.S. 2, where you will see the Iron River Tourist Information Welcome Center and the RV park. Parking is available at a small parking lot along River Avenue to the right of the trail.

Iron River to the Wisconsin border

The final section of the State Line runs 21.2 miles from Iron River to the Wisconsin border. A few trail segments have temporary closures to motorized vehicles between September 1 and December 1—watch your calendar if you are traveling by motorized transport.

Starting in Iron River, then passing through Stambaugh and Caspian, this section will give you more of a workout than others—at least initially. Once you get out of the wood chips, the trail has deep ruts from ATV traffic for about the first mile. Soon after, you will come to a fork; stay to the right and to the right again at the second fork, and then cross the bridge. The trail parallels the Iron River, and you will pass a wooden walkway that canoeists use for portage over a section of rapids. Keep going through this developed area, past an old mine, through a commercial area in Caspian and past a service drive to a treatment plant. Finally, you will reach tranquility.

About 0.6 miles into tranquility (about three miles into the start of this trail section), you get to the first gate that closes off motorized traffic in the fall months. You will notice many ferns, wildflowers and birch trees lining the trail's perimeter. After the trail veers to the left, rolling farmland envelops the trail until you reach the second gate that closes off this section.

The next 4.7 miles (not restricted to motorized use) continue through farmland, pass through birch and aspen and then veer to the left. A land bridge slopes steeply to the river—be careful, the trail is covered with loose rock. As you continue on, you get occasional glimpses of the river on the right. With any luck, you will get a peek at some osprey on the constructed platform.

A half-mile past the osprey platform is a dirt road crossing. Beyond it, a gate closes off motorized vehicles again for about two miles. After the final gate, Mastedon Township Park is 6.2 miles away. This portion takes you over land bridges and bridges with scenic overlooks and also past two more osprey nesting platforms. When you will reach the park, you may want to use the restrooms, picnic tables, barbecue grills and swing set. The park, which is a good starting or stopping point, also has access to Stager Lake and day parking.

If you want to continue on, the Michigan/Wisconsin border is 1.7 miles away, where you will find a bridge linking the two states over Brule River. Take a few minutes to try to spot a bald eagle.

On the Wisconsin side, the trail currently is used only for snowmobiling. However, the Wisconsin Department of Transportation foresees the potential acquisition of it for multiple use, which would link the trail through Wisconsin.

Children enjoy Michigan's only existing rail-trail with an adjacent active railroad line—the Traverse Area Recreational Trail.

Traverse Area Recreational Trail
(TART)

Endpoints: Traverse City

Location: Grand Traverse County

Length: 2.4 miles

Surface: Asphalt

Uses:

Contact: Mike Dillenbeck, Manager
Grand Traverse County Road Commission
3949 Silver Lake Road
Traverse City, MI 49684
626-922-4848

◆◆◆

Known primarily as a tourist mecca and as the Tart Cherry Capital of the World, Traverse City also holds the unique distinction as home to Michigan's only rails-WITH-trail project—a trail that shares a corridor with an active railroad.

One of about 20 successfully operating "rails-with-trails" across the country, the Traverse Area Recreational Trail is located a fair distance from the active line and is separated by a fence.

The trail starts east of Boardman Lake on Barlow, south of East Eighth Street. Parking is available at the abandoned railroad depot on the northeast end of the lake. From the parking lot, head east 0.2 miles along a dirt road to where the asphalt trail begins.

While the trail along this section is not very scenic, it provides an important function of serving local needs. It is a good example of a community using available resources to provide a safe non-motorized facility. The trail currently ends at Three Mile Road.

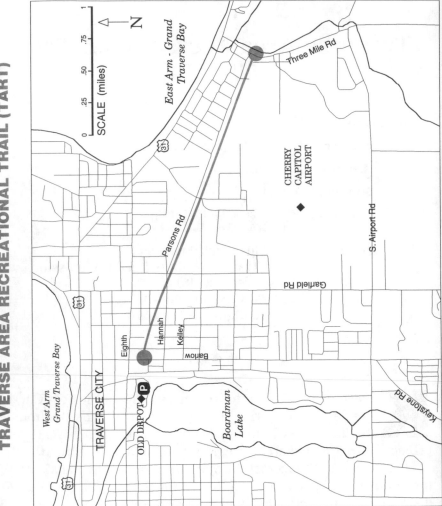

TRAVERSE AREA RECREATIONAL TRAIL (TART)

When finished (scheduled for 1994), the trail will pass through more scenic landscape and will provide a safe route from the downtown area to the Grand Traverse Resort. It also will complete the first step in the development of a network of non-motorized trails in and around the Traverse City area.

Watersmeet/Land O' Lakes Trail

Endpoints: Watersmeet to Land O' Lakes, Wisconsin

Location: Gogebic County

Length: 8.8 miles

Surface: Dirt, gravel, sand and original ballast

Uses: 🚶 🚲 🐎 🎣 🛷 🏍️

Contact: Wayne Petterson, District Ranger
U.S. Forest Service
P. O. Box 276
Watersmeet, MI 49969
906-358-4551

❖ ❖ ❖

This trail begins where waters meet, then flows south to the land o' lakes. The Watersmeet area is home to more than 300 lakes, including the Cisco Chain of 15 lakes. It also hosts more than 240 miles of trout streams as well as the Sylvania Wilderness and Recreation Area that encompasses more than 21,000 acres of virgin forest. And Land O' Lakes, well, it's just that.

This rugged trail, following Duck Creek most of its way, attracts the suspecting and unsuspecting with its stands of tall pines (occasionally growing right up to the corridor), its fern-carpeted forest floors, its ponds and beaver huts and its potential for viewing eagles and other wildlife. The intermittent sand, occasional railroad relics and periodic protruding rocks only hasten to ensnare the adventurer.

The Michigan Department of Natural Resources has been working to improve this trail by redecking some bridges and opening it

WATERSMEET/LAND O' LAKES TRAIL

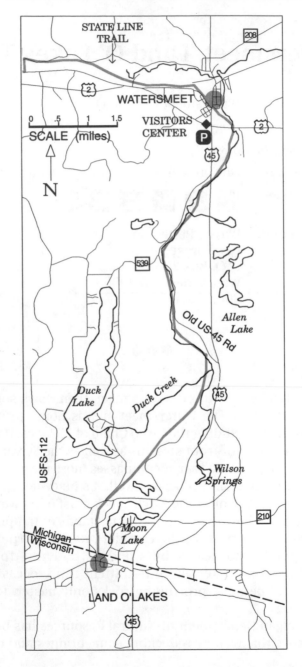

up to less-ambitious travelers. But, the experience is not diminished.

Parking is available at the Watersmeet Visitor's Center for the Ottawa National Forest on U.S. 2 and M-45. Plan to visit the center's nature exhibits and to browse through the available information, maps and brochures. You can also park at the pavilion in town where the railroad roundhouse once existed.

The trail starts on the west side of State Route 45 at the north end of Watersmeet, where the Watersmeet/Land O' Lakes Trail meets the State Line Trail (see page 107). It parallels M-45 for about a quarter-mile, before crossing M-45 to the left, then continues for an additional quarter-mile before dipping under U.S. 2.

From this point, all you need to do is enjoy this lush trail until it ends in Land O' Lakes, Wisconsin. You cannot miss the end: the

Lush scenery surrounds much of the Watersmeet/Land O' Lakes Trail.

Land O' Lakes Library is built smack in the middle of the corridor.

As long as your are not in a designated campground, hikers, canoeists or others can camp in the Ottawa National Forest without a permit. However, do not cut down any live trees or plants, make sure campfires are out before leaving your campsite and pack out your trash.

West Bloomfield Trail Network

Endpoints: West Bloomfield Woods Nature Preserve to Sylvan Manor Park in West Bloomfield

Location: Oakland County

Length: 4.25 miles

Surface: Crushed stone

Uses:

Contact: Ms. Joey Spano, Director
West Bloomfield Parks and Recreation
3325 Middlebelt Road
West Bloomfield, MI 48323
313-334-5660

◆ ◆ ◆

W hen the Michigan Air Line Railroad built its rail line through West Bloomfield in the late 1870s, little did it know that part of the line would later be an air line for great blue herons.

With the era of steam and smoke long gone and the era of auto dependency ever present, you, along with these majestic birds, can seek refuge along the 4.25-mile linear greenway. This so-called "Emerald Necklace" pays tribute not only to the past, but also to a community that fought hard to preserve this route, and to communities—both human and wild—that flock to it.

The starting point at Arrowhead Road, south of Pontiac Trail, serves as the west trailhead to the trail network and as the access point to the West Bloomfield Woods Nature Preserve. This 162-acre preserve was Michigan's first location to receive national recognition as an Urban Wildlife Sanctuary. It hosts more than 100 bird

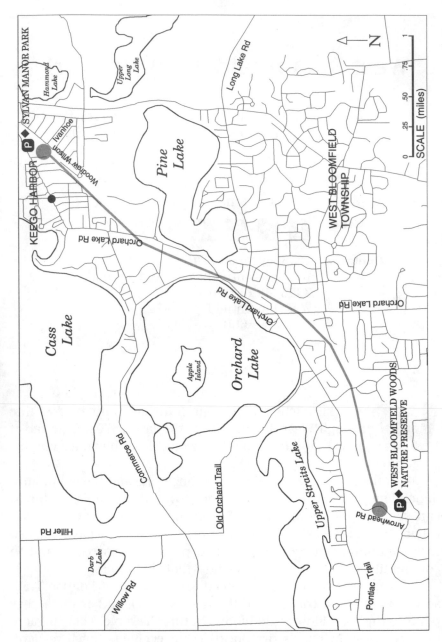

WEST BLOOMFIELD TRAIL NETWORK

SYLVAN MANOR PARK

Hammond Lake

Upper Long Lake

Long Lake Rd

Ivanhoe

Woodrow Wilson

KEEGO HARBOR

Pine Lake

Orchard Lake Rd

WEST BLOOMFIELD TOWNSHIP

Cass Lake

Apple Island

Orchard Lake

Orchard Lake Rd

Orchard Lake Rd

Commerce Rd

Hiller Rd

Old Orchard Trail

Upper Straits Lake

Darb Lake

Willow Rd

Arrowhead Rd

WEST BLOOMFIELD WOODS NATURE PRESERVE

Pontiac Trail

N

SCALE (miles)

0 .25 .50 .75 1

Judith Share-Vine

Take a few moments to view the Blue Heron nesting area along the trail.

species and a great blue heron rookery. It also serves as home to red fox, mink, weasel, white-tailed deer and blue-spotted salamander. Take some time to wander through the preserve along the half-mile, wheelchair accessible trail or the 2.1-mile wood-chipped nature trail.

Back on the grade, you don't have to travel far before you get to the overlook for the great blue heron rookery—you will hear the squawks before you see the overlook, especially in springtime. Look up and enjoy what is nestled in the trees.

Travel a short stretch down the trail and you will understand why the preserve was designated an Urban Wildlife Sanctuary (especially when you try crossing the trail as it cuts across Orchard Lake Road a few times). Interspersed among the lakes and wooded wetlands are condominiums, palatial homes and shopping centers at the busy road crossings. All serve as constant reminders that this narrow slice of nature is indeed a sanctuary from its urban environs—for wildlife as well as humans.

Shortly after passing through the tunnel under Long Lake Road, look over your left shoulder and you will see Orchard Lake across the road, where (according to rumor) Chief Pontiac is buried on Apple Island. The island is a roosting spot for blackbirds and a hunting ground for hawks, owls and blue herons.

The trail winds down at the Sylvan Manor Park after passing through the communities of West Bloomfield, Orchard Lake, Keego Harbor and Sylvan Lake. The three-acre park offers a softball diamond, basketball court, play area and picnic area with grills—a fitting clasp to the "Emerald Necklace."

An Introduction to Rail-Trails in Illinois

With nearly 25 rail-trails totaling more than 325 miles, Illinois is a great state for trail enthusiasts! A front-runner in the rail-trail movement, Illinois is home to the 55-mile Illinois Prairie Path— one of the trails credited with initiating the national rails-to-trails movement.

It should come as no surprise that a state with so much railroad history would create one of the nation's first rail-trails. In the late 1800s, Chicago was the crossroads of the railroad industry, and the state of Illinois was crisscrossed with thousands of miles of rails. At the peak of the railroading era, the state boasted more than 12,000 miles of track. Now, more than 4,000 of those miles have been abandoned, most of it since the 1960s.

The citizens of Illinois were not willing to let their industrial heritage disappear, nor did they want all of their open space consumed by the steady sprawl of Chicago.

In 1963, naturalist May Theilgaard Watts addressed both issues in a letter to the editor of the *Chicago Tribune*, proposing constructive reuse of an abandoned railroad outside of Chicago. Her practical letter led to the creation of the Illinois Prairie Path and ignited a movement to save rail corridors for use as multi-use, public trails.

Two dozen trails now extend throughout Illinois, which became the second state chapter of Rails-to-Trails Conservancy. Formed in 1987, the Illinois Chapter has had an office in Springfield since 1989 supporting legislative efforts, providing technical assistance to rail-trail projects and increasing the public's awareness of trails in Illinois.

This book highlights the best trails in Illinois. Whether your journeys take you near the "Windy City" of Chicago, to the outskirts of St. Louis or to the more rural areas of the state, this book will provide interesting trail experiences. Happy Trails!

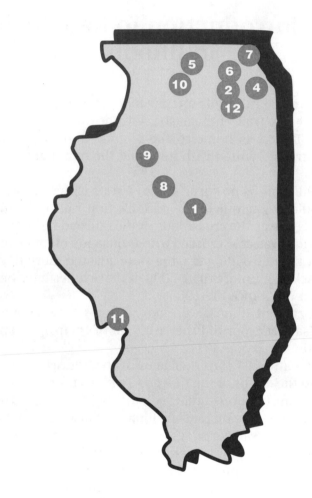

ILLINOIS' GREAT RAIL-TRAILS

1. Constitution Trail

2. Fox River Trail

3. Great Western Trail

4. Illinois Prairie Path

5. Long Prairie Trail

6. McHenry County Prairie Trail (South)

7. North Shore Bike Path

8. River Trail of Illinois

9. Rock Island Trail State Park

10. Rock River Recreation Path

11. Vadalabene Great River Road Bike Trail

12. Virgil L. Gilman Nature Trail

Constitution Trail

Endpoints: Bloomington to Normal

Location: McLean County

Length: 5.3 Miles

Surface: Asphalt

Uses:

Contact: Keith Rich, Director
Bloomington Parks and Recreation
Department
109 East Olive Street
Bloomington, IL 61701
309-823-4260

The Constitution Trail runs through residential neighborhoods and occasional patches of prairie as well as near business areas and two universities, all of which create an appealing setting for a wide variety of users.

The final mile of the Constitution Trail, which runs from Emerson Street south to Washington Street in Bloomington, was completed in the fall of 1993. Beginning at Washington Street, the trail heads north toward Normal. No specific trailhead parking exists, but parking on side streets is allowable as long as you pay attention to signs that restrict parking.

As you head north, the trail runs through neighborhoods and near small commercial areas. While all road crossings on this section of trail are at-grade, few of the streets have much traffic. As always, watch for cars at these crossings.

CONSTITUTION TRAIL

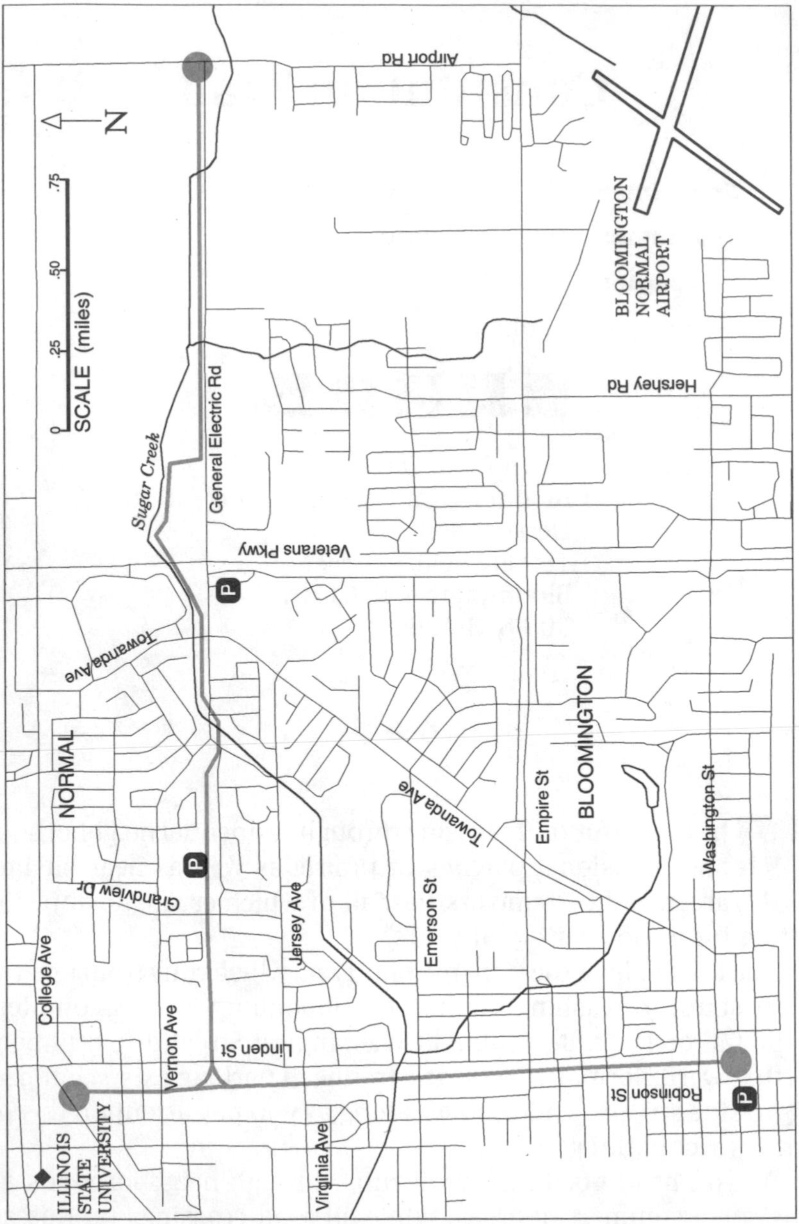

SCALE (miles)

0 .25 .50 .75

N

Airport Rd

BLOOMINGTON
NORMAL
AIRPORT

Hershey Rd

Sugar Creek

General Electric Rd

Veterans Pkwy

Towanda Ave

NORMAL

Grandview Dr

College Ave

Vernon Ave

Linden St

Jersey Ave

Virginia Ave

Towanda Ave

Emerson St

Empire St

BLOOMINGTON

Washington St

Robinson St

ILLINOIS
STATE
UNIVERSITY

Native prairie borders the trail.

The trail crosses over busy Emerson street on a bridge, followed closely by a crossing over Sugar creek. As you continue north under Camelback Bridge, you will come to a split in the trail.

One segment of trail continues north for less than a half-mile to downtown Normal. The trail passes over another branch of Sugar Creek on a high embankment, then crosses Vernon Avenue. From here you will travel a short distance to Phoenix Street, just off Broadway, where the trail's northern segment ends just a few blocks from the campus of Illinois State University.

The other segment veers east, quickly passes over Linden Street and continues toward Grandview Drive. Benches and picnic tables are available along the trail and parking is available at Colene Hoose School, just off Grandview Drive. The trail continues east until it reaches Vernon Avenue, where it moves onto the sidewalk for a short distance, then crosses the street at a marked crossing.

After crossing Vernon, the trail passes through a small park-like area adjacent to Sugar Creek, where benches, picnic tables, portable toilets and water fountains are available. You also will find several restaurants and convenience stores in the area. As the trail continues east, it passes under Towanda Avenue, behind several buildings and under Veterans Parkway.

Illinois Governor Jim Edgar

Illinois Governor Jim Edgar is a strong trail supporter and often takes time out to enjoy a bike ride. He played a major role in creating and funding the Illinois Bike Path Program when he served as the Secretary of State.

The Bike Path Grant Program assists local agencies with trail development. Bike Path Grants provide up to 50 percent of an approved project's total cost. Since the program's inception in 1989, $11.5 million has been appropriated to fund 280 miles of trails throughout Illinois.

Governor Edgar (center) rides down the Constitution Trail after announcing the 1994 Illinois Bike Path Grant Awards. Bloomington Mayor Jesse Smart (left) and Department of Conservation Director Brent Manning accompany the Governor.

You will quickly find yourself in a field of prairie grass, which offers a quiet refuge from the traffic on Veterans Parkway. Or, if you prefer, take a detour to nearby shops at College Hills Mall or Lakewood Plaza. From the prairie field, the trail veers right along General Electric Progress Park, then parallels General Electric Road until it reaches its easternmost terminus at Airport Road. Several access points are located along this section of the trail as well as benches and a shelter near Airport Road.

A local garden project adds a pleasant backdrop to the popular Fox River Trail.

Fox River Trail

Endpoints: Algonquin to Aurora

Location: Kane County

Length: 33 miles

Surface: Primarily asphalt, with a few pockets of crushed limestone

Uses:

(in designated areas)

Contacts: Jon J. Duerr, Superintendent
Kane County Forest Preserve
719 Batavia Avenue
Geneva, IL 60134
708-232-5981

Charles E. Hoscheit, Director
Fox Valley Park District
712 South River Street
Aurora, IL 60507
708-897-0516

◆◆◆

This scenic recreational trail parallels the Fox River for most of its length, linking together a variety of historic towns and local parks. The Fox River Trail offers numerous access points; if you are up for a long trip, you can start just north of the Kane County line and go south (with the flow of the river) all the way to Aurora.

The town of Algonquin, filled with Victorian-style buildings, sits just north of the McHenry/Kane County line. On-street parking is

FOX RIVER TRAIL

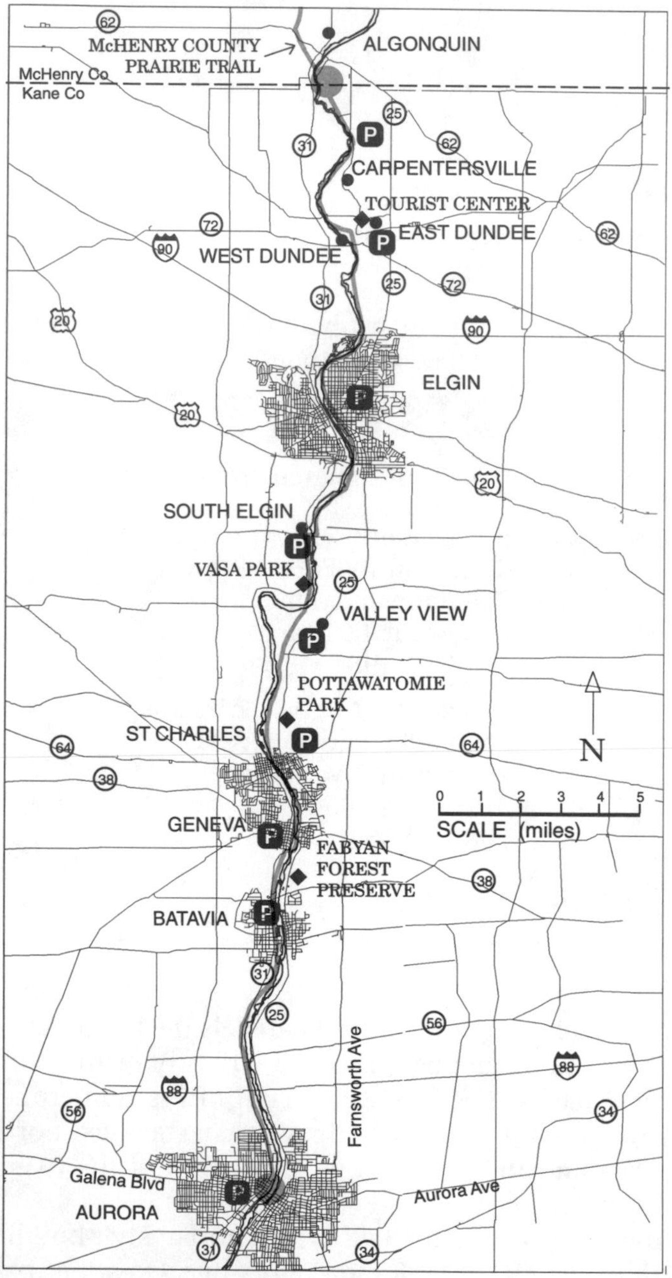

62

McHENRY COUNTY
PRAIRIE TRAIL

McHenry Co
Kane Co

ALGONQUIN

31   25   62

CARPENTERSVILLE

TOURIST CENTER

72   EAST DUNDEE   62

90   WEST DUNDEE

31   25   72

90

ELGIN

20

20

SOUTH ELGIN

VASA PARK   25

VALLEY VIEW

POTTAWATOMIE
PARK

ST CHARLES   64

64   N

0 1 2 3 4 5
SCALE (miles)

38

GENEVA

FABYAN
FOREST
PRESERVE   38

BATAVIA

31

25   56

88   Farnsworth Ave   88

56   34

Galena Blvd   Aurora Ave

AURORA

31   34

fairly plentiful in Algonquin—the best bet is side streets off Illinois State Route 31 (Main Street). The McHenry County Prairie Trail (see page 159) crosses Illinois 31 just south of State Route 62. The best landmark for finding the rail-trail is the Prairie Path Bike Shop, located adjacent to the trail at Railroad Street and State Route 31.

You will enter the trail on the east side of Route 31, cross the Fox River, and within a half-mile you will be on the Fox River Trail. No signs mark the official dividing line, which is Souwanas Street.

This northern section of the trail leads through a residential area, which soon leads back to the river, and within a mile reaches the Fox River Shores Forest Preserve. Next you will reach a string of small, once-industrial towns along the river. The first one is Carpentersville, a former steel manufacturing center, followed quickly by East Dundee, which initially served as an industrial area with its extensive brick-making facilities. Parking is available in East Dundee near the Dundee Township Tourist Center.

The Fox River Trail, which offers a more natural setting and some native prairie species once you leave East Dundee, is home to an ingenious river crossing under Interstate 90. Using the support structure of the highway, an exclusive trail bridge has been developed to carry trail users over the river and under the Interstate. The bridge leads to a mile-long trail on the west side of the Fox River, which will take you to the Tyler Creek Forest Preserve.

If you opt not to take the side trip, the next "destination" along the Fox River Trail is Elgin, where the trail is primarily on-street. At the Elgin Marine Club, follow bike route signs across a double set of railroad tracks onto North Grove Avenue. Proceed on-road for just under a mile; turn west onto Kimball Street; and, prior to crossing the river, turn south onto the Fox River Trail. A large, public parking lot is located nearby.

In two miles (after crossing under Route 20) you will come to a three-block "detour" beginning at Raymond Avenue. The county plans to install a bridge over the series of heavily-used railroad tracks, but until that happens, take Raymond Avenue carefully across the railroad tracks and then back to the trail at Purify Road.

Just after you re-enter the trail, you will come to a fork in the trail. The one that veers to the right, under the railroad tracks and along the river is the continuation of the Fox River Trail. The one veering to the left is the west end of the Illinois Prairie Path's Elgin

Spur (see page 146). The first Prairie Path sign appears after the spur crosses Raymond Avenue, where a 20-car parking lot is located.

You will remain on the east side of the Fox River until South Elgin, where you will cross to the river's west side via State Street. You will parallel the river's west side for a little more than a mile until you reach Vasa Park. This lush, green setting along the river offers numerous picnic tables, a boat launch, restrooms, a shelter and ample parking.

Do not take the paved trail heading out of Vasa Park, it is simply a new access trail for the developing communities in Valley View. To continue on the Fox River Trail, take the long bridge span back across the Fox River; go up a steep hill, past a small Forest Preserve parking lot, across the street and onto a sidewalk that runs next to the Anderson School. You will go downhill on Weber Drive (no bike lane) until just before Pearson Drive, where the trail again becomes a separated path and begins to head back toward the river. You will be on-street again for a short stretch between the intersections of Grove and Rockwell and Grove and Sunset.

Railroad relics create an interesting sculpture near Geneva.

The river is quite wide and scenic where you resume traveling along its banks. The floods in the summer of 1993 caused some erosion in this area, but the tall trees, abundant wildlife and peaceful setting make up for the trail's occasional inconsistent surface. After winding through the Norris Woods Nature Preserve, the separated trail ends on 3rd Street, indicating your approach into St. Charles. At this point, you are beyond the halfway point between Algonquin and Aurora.

You will continue on 3rd Street for a little more than a mile and then carefully follow bike route signs into downtown St. Charles—home to many old-style Victorian buildings and a fair bit of road construction. After several possible detours, the trail cuts between State Route 25 (Riverside Drive) and the Fox River as you head south toward Geneva—except for a short loop around a water treatment plant. In this area, the trail often is referred to as the Riverside Trail.

The trail meanders along the river on some well-worn asphalt and takes on the feel of a sidewalk as you near Geneva, which has several shops, restaurants and a bike shop. If you prefer a quiet picnic, continue on the trail under Illinois Route 38, and you will enter Island Park. Here—amidst abundant weeping willows—you can enjoy a picnic, view a sculpture, feed the mallards or just enjoy the scenery on this island within the Fox River.

Soon after leaving Island Park, you will see another ingenious river crossing—built exclusively for trail users—that uses the support structure of the active railroad overhead. If you continue on the east side of the Fox River, you will reach the Fabyan Forest Preserve within a mile. Here, you will find restrooms, picnic tables, a seasonal snack shop and plenty of parking.

Heading south from this point, the Fox River Trail basically runs on both sides of the river until State Street in North Aurora, although the only places to cross the river are in Batavia and North Aurora. You may want to consider creating a loop out of various portions of the trail.

One highlight, the Red Oak Nature Center, is located along the east bank of the Fox River. The trail skirts the edge of the nature center, which is a popular family destination. Here, you will find an 80-acre area with excellent interpretive signing, a full-time staff naturalist and several hiking trails.

Dundee Township Tourist Center

The Tourist Center is housed in a reconstructed train depot.

If your trip includes the northern portion of the Fox River Trail, be sure to take advantage of the Dundee Township Tourist Center, located four miles south of Algonquin in a recon- structed, mint-green train depot next to the trail—it caters al- most exclusively to trail users.

Not only does the knowledgeably-staffed Center provide restrooms, cold water and low-priced snacks, it also offers a host of trail maps and other regional information. Possibly the best purchase you can make is the Fox Valley Trail Guide map and the accompanying mileage chart. The center developed this much-needed mileage guide for the extensive Fox River Trail system.

Some original railroad-related structures remain in East Dundee, located across from the visitors center. In addition, several antique shops and restaurants are located in the quaint town.

From State Street in North Aurora to Illinois Avenue in down-town Aurora, the trail is located only on the west side of the Fox River. You will know that you have reached Illinois Avenue when you see the attractive Veteran's Island and the Veterans Memorial on the east bank of the river, where parking is available. The sculpture was dedicated on Memorial Day in 1991. From here, you can pick up the Aurora Spur of the Illinois Prairie Path (see page 146).

For a short stretch south from Illinois Street to New York Street, the Fox Valley Park District has developed the Fox River Trail on both sides of the river. The current southern terminus is located at North River Street Park, which is across from the Aurora Police Station and Courthouse just north of New York Street. The paddleboat from Aurora's Riverboat Gambling Casino often is situated on the Fox River in front of this park. The new gambling craze in Aurora has brought with it numerous public parking lots and garages, so parking in Aurora will rarely be a problem.

The Fox Valley Park District is completing its plans to continue the trail almost another two miles to Montgomery, near the Kane/Kendall County border. This connection will intersect with the Virgil L. Gilman Nature Trail where it crosses the Fox River in Aurora—yet another link in the vast rail-trail network in the western suburbs of Chicago.

Setting the pace along the Fox River Trail.

The start of the Great Western Trail in St. Charles

Great Western Trail

Endpoints:	St. Charles to Sycamore
Location:	Kane and DeKalb Counties
Length:	18 miles
Surface:	Primarily crushed stone, with pockets of asphalt
Uses:	
	🏇 (in designated areas)
Contacts:	Jon Duerr, Superintendent Kane County Forest Preserve 719 Batavia Avenue Geneva, IL 60134 708-232-5981
	Terry Hannan, Superintendent Dekalb County Forest Preserve 110 East Sycamore Street Sycamore, IL 60178 815-895-7191

◆◆◆

Generally considered a remote and rural area, western Kane County is currently experiencing rapid residential development that is gradually changing the nature of the Great Western Trail. However, if you are looking to "get away from it all," the Great Western Trail probably remains the most rural of the suburban Chicago rail-trails.

To access the trailhead, take Illinois State Route 64 west from St. Charles to Randall Road north; signs lead you to the trail's park-

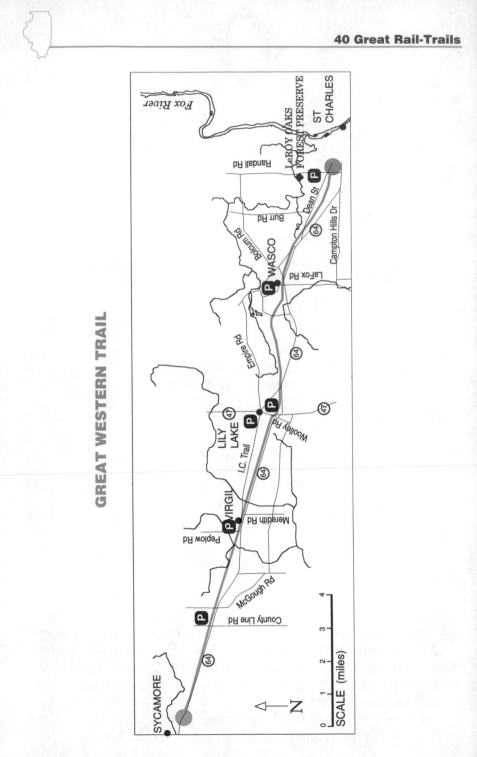

GREAT WESTERN TRAIL

SYCAMORE

County Line Rd

McGough Rd

Peplow Rd

VIRGIL

Meredith Rd

LILY
LAKE

I.C. Trail

Woolley Rd

Empire Rd

WASCO

LaFox Rd

Baldwin Rd

Burr Rd

Randall Rd

LeROY OAKS
FOREST PRESERVE

Dean St

Campton Hills Dr

ST
CHARLES

Fox River

64

47

47

64

64

64

N

SCALE (miles)

0 1 2 3 4

ing lot on the west side of the street. The well-developed trailhead includes abundant parking, a large picnic shelter, restrooms and a kiosk.

As you embark on the trail heading west, the trail basically cuts between farmland dotted with occasional residences. The trail is shrouded in trees, giving it the sense of a true linear park. The well-packed crushed limestone changes to intermittent stretches of asphalt, typically before and after any road crossings. Fortunately, many of the crossings are grade-separated with bridges.

Restrooms are available at the Wasco Road crossing, approximately four miles west of the trailhead. Pockets of new developments are occasionally noticeable on alternating sides of the trail, which remains fairly isolated as it winds through the gently rolling landscape.

The next small town along the route, Lily Lake, is just shy of the trail's halfway point. After crossing State Route 47, you take a short jaunt on Woolley Road south to Route 64, where you can see the town's hot dog carry out (and picnic tables) as well as the gas station mini-mart. Between Lily Lake and Virgil (just over four miles), the trail closely parallels Route 64, although a band of trees and the now-rural landscape helps to minimize the road's impact.

In Virgil, where you can stop for restrooms and refreshments, the trail veers slightly northwest, offering a respite from Route 64. When the road approaches the trail again, you are about to cross into definitively rural DeKalb County for the trail's last two miles.

The Great Western Trail ends on the outskirts of Sycamore, the DeKalb County Seat, at the intersection of State Route 64 and Old State Street. At this point, you are less than a mile from a few fast-food restaurants and a grocery store and less than 1.5 miles from historic downtown Sycamore. If you have the time, it's worth the trip just to see the old-fashioned Main Street architecture and the attractive County Courthouse.

Kevin C. Menke

Kids enjoy the multiple uses of the Illinois Prairie Path

Illinois Prairie Path

Endpoints: Maywood to Wheaton with spurs to Aurora, Batavia and Elgin

Location: Cook, DuPage and Kane Counties

Length: 55 miles

Surface: primarily crushed stone, with some asphalt and dirt

Uses:

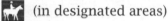 (in designated areas)

Contacts: Jean Mooring
Illinois Prairie Path, Inc.
P.O. Box 1086
Wheaton, IL 60189
708-665-5310

Charles Tokarski
DuPage County Division of Transportation
130 North County Farm Road
Wheaton, IL 60187
708-682-7318

Charles E. Hoscheit, Director
Fox Valley Park District
P.O. Box 818
Aurora, IL 60507
708-897-0516

◆◆◆

elebrated as one of the trails that sparked the entire rails-to-trails movement, this seemingly endless trail is one of the best things that ever happened to Chicago's western

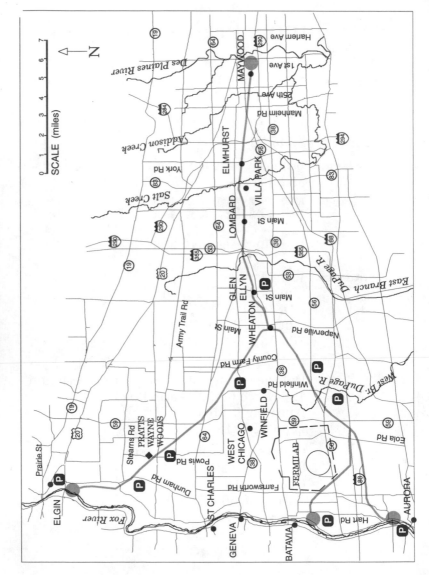

ILLINOIS PRAIRIE PATH

suburbs. Without one woman's vision and dozens of committed volunteers, the Illinois Prairie Path never would have been built.

In 1963, May Theilgaard Watts wrote an inspirational letter to the *Chicago Tribune* calling for the former Chicago, Aurora and Elgin Electric Railway to be converted into a public trail.

"We are human beings. We are able to walk upright on two feet. We need a footpath," wrote Watts, a distinguished naturalist and avid hiker. "Right now there is a chance for Chicago and its suburbs to have a footpath, a long one. The right of way lies waiting. If we have the courage and foresight...we can create from this strip a proud resource."

Her words, which motivated a group of volunteers to form Illinois Prairie Path, Inc., could not have been more accurate. Shaped like a sideways pitchfork and stretching more than 50 miles, this trail is a beautiful and constantly-pleasant respite from the never-ending sprawl of Chicago's western suburbs.

The shape of this trail offers virtually limitless opportunities for possible starting and ending points; however, be aware that this trail is generally considered a "local" trail, so parking is extremely limited along most of the trail's route.

Crossing one of the trail's many bridges

Wheaton is the heart of the trail, where the two primary spurs and the trail's stem converge. From Wheaton, you can travel east, paralleling active tracks and several quaint downtown "main streets" for much of the 15 miles to Maywood. Or, you could travel 15 miles northwest to Elgin, where you could pick up the Fox River Trail near its northern terminus (see page 134). Or, you could travel southwest 12 miles to Aurora, where you can pick up the Fox River Trail near its southern terminus. From the Aurora spur, you can also pick up the six-mile Batavia Spur.

For any of these options, you should begin your journey at the Prairie Path trailhead in downtown Wheaton, located at the intersection of Liberty Street and Carlton Avenue, just north of Illinois State Route 38 (Roosevelt Road). A limestone sign and an interesting sculpture made from remnants of the original rail line welcome you to the Illinois Prairie Path. At the corner, you also will find a municipal parking lot—only open to the public on weekends—as well as metered street parking.

Wheaton to Maywood

Downtown Wheaton, with its "mainstreet USA" feel, offers a mix of quaint shops and restaurants. Heading east, the trail runs along the sidewalk for couple of short stretches before becoming a separated limestone path. After passing the Wheaton mass transit station, you will find Founders Park, a small grassy knoll anchored with a large stone commemorating May Theilgaard Watts.

The trail parallels two active rail lines for the first four miles, until they veer away from the trail in Glen Ellyn. Soon you will reach a fairly dangerous diagonal at-grade road crossing after passing a sign that says, "Slow, Path Narrows." Use caution as motorists are not alerted with any signs or a crosswalk. The next "crossing" takes you on a long bridge over Interstate 355 and then back into a more residential setting.

After the five-mile mark, you cross over Main Street in Lombard, another in a string of historic downtown areas offering shops and restaurants. The next one is Villa Park, which is home to the Illinois Prairie Path Visitors Center and the Historical Society Museum. They are housed together in a former rail station—stop in for information, restrooms and water. At mile marker 8, just before the State Route 83 overpass, you will pass the now-defunct Ovaltine Plant,

Gathering wildflower seeds along the Illinois Prairie Path

which produced a malted milk drink for more than 60 years, beginning in 1917. The adjacent town of Elmhurst offers a restaurant or two as well as a bike shop prior to the Interstate 294 underpass.

Beyond mile marker 12, the trail is not developed and the surface is gravel (where the corridor is not completely overgrown). While the trail is generally hikeable and passable on mountain bike, the

Jogging across Volunteer Bridge

surroundings are not very appealing. Somewhat hard to follow, the trail goes under a number of underpasses and through a much more industrial setting to its terminus at First Street in Maywood.

Elgin Spur

From the Wheaton trailhead (at Liberty Street and Carlton Avenue), you will take the asphalt path over the active rail lines on an iron truss railroad bridge known as "Volunteer Bridge" because it was reconstructed completely through a volunteer citizen effort in 1983.

The trail quickly heads off into a surprisingly natural setting for suburban Chicago. In less than a mile from Volunteer Bridge, you will arrive at the Lincoln Marsh Natural Area, where a rounded overlook affords beautiful views of wetlands and restored habitat. Just beyond the overlook, a (wheelchair accessible) ramp leads to a series of nature trails through the marshes. Bicycles are prohibited on the trails.

For the next few miles, the Prairie Path is quite serene, with a canopy of trees overhead. One major at-grade road crossing (the corner of County Farm and Geneva Roads) breaks up the scenery, but signaled crosswalks ease you through the traffic. This intersection is home of the Prairie Trail Shopping Center, where you will find several shops and restaurants. Soon you cut through the Timber Ridge Preserve where deer and other wildlife are prevalent.

Beyond Prince Crossing Road (just prior to mile marker 5), the limestone surface tends to be a bit sandy and soft, and then the trail abruptly comes to a steep staircase that leads up to former rail line converted into a utility corridor. Another staircase (and a steep, non-accessible, ramp) lead to the continuation of the Prairie Path. An underpass takes you under busy Illinois Route 64, and after passing a shopping center, a new bridge takes you over equally-busy Illinois Route 59.

For the next couple of miles, the trail runs between various residential neighborhoods, although the trees lining the route often make you feel pleasantly isolated. Between mile markers 9 and 11, the trail cuts through Pratts Wayne Woods Forest Preserve before crossing over Route 25 and returning to a rural-residential setting.

The Elgin Spur of the Illinois Prairie Path "ends" in Elgin when it intersects with the paved Fox River Trail just after crossing over Raymond Avenue and passing a small parking lot. In fact, you may not even realize the Prairie Path has ended (there are no signs), but you will come to a "Y" in the trail. One section heads under a set of railroad tracks toward the Fox River and the other is temporarily diverted on-street, over three active railroad tracks. Both are the Fox River Trail, which continues north to Algonquin and south to Aurora (see page 134).

Aurora and Batavia Spurs

The Aurora Spur also begins at the Wheaton trailhead. Initially, the trail runs along the sidewalk of Carlton Avenue, although signs indicate that it doubles as the Illinois Prairie Path. Within a quarter of a mile, you will cross Roosevelt Avenue (State Route 38) and head onto the Path. For about a mile, the Prairie Path runs between a series of recently-developed homes, many of which advertised their proximity to the trail while they were on the market.

Soon the trail's surroundings temporarily take on a more rural, less developed feel as the trail skirts a series of nature preserves and then crosses under State Route 56. In less than two miles, you will approach Interstate 88 (the East-West Tollway). As you cross under State Route 59 and reach the intersection with Ferry Road, the trail splits into two sections: one is the start of the Batavia Spur and the other is the continuation of the Aurora Spur.

The Batavia Spur begins by heading west, paralleling the Interstate for more than two miles. Initially the trail is about 100 feet below the highway, although both routes gradually level out to almost the same level. Fortunately, this rather noisy scenario doesn't last for long. Just before reaching the DuPage/Kane County border, the trail heads northwest toward Batavia, where it meets up with the Fox River Trail (see page 134) after crossing under State Route 25.

The Aurora Spur continues in its southwesterly route, first passing under the Interstate and then passing by a massive power sub-station, which emits a string of unsightly power lines. The two-mile stretch of high tension lines, coupled with the light-industrial setting, make this one of the least memorable sections of the Prairie Path.

The trail ends within another mile at a large trail parking lot along the Fox River, a block west of State Route 25. Across Illinois Avenue, you will see the attractive Veteran's Memorial Park. From here, you can pick up the paved Fox River Trail East, a new segment of the Fox River Trail, which you can pick up on the west side of river.

If you want to take a break, you will find numerous restaurants and fast food chains as well as a grocery store on the west side of the Fox River. Or, if you need any bicycle supplies, you will find a bike shop at the corner of Illinois Avenue and Route 25—a block from the trail terminus.

Long Prairie Trail

Endpoints: McHenry County Line to State Route 76

Location: Boone County

Length: 9.5 miles

Surface: Asphalt

Uses: 🚶 🚲 ♿ ⛷ 🛼

Contact: Boone County Conservation District
7600 Appleton Road
Belvidere, IL 61008
815-547-7935

◆ ◆ ◆

C urrently, the Long Prairie Trail runs more than halfway across rural Boone County. Plans call for the trail to continue west approximately eight miles to Winnebago County, where the more rustic Stone Bridge Trail will continue on the same corridor to the Wisconsin border. The Natural Land Institute recently acquired that line for a nature trail in Winnebago County.

The Long Prairie Trail begins at a parking lot on County Line Road located a half-mile north of Illinois Route 173. One of the trail's interesting features is a series of markers that describe both the natural and human history of the area. You will find the first marker in the parking lot, describing the Potawatomi Tribe, which moved through the area prior to European settlement.

From the parking lot the trail heads toward the town of Capron, which was settled after the Kenosha, Rockford and Rock Island Railroad Company began laying tracks in 1858. After a few street crossings, you cut through a parking lot. Here, you will find another

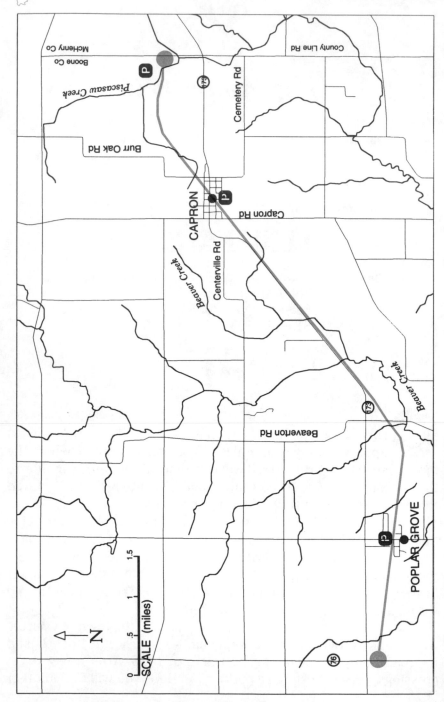

LONG PRAIRIE TRAIL

Learning how to in-line skate on the Long Prairie Trail

marker describing the history of Capron, which was once known as Helgesaw and then Long Prairie.

From this lot, the trail crosses a couple of streets before paralleling Route 173 for about three miles. Additional markers found along this section of trail explain the area's natural features: peat bogs, fens and prairies. A discussion of glaciers is particularly interesting, as they created the land that the Long Prairie Trail traverses.

The trail continues through gently rolling terrain, away from Route 173 and around a curve and to another marker detailing the railroad that once used the corridor. You can also learn about a train accident that occurred at this location, destroying the tracks and putting an end to train traffic on the line. A gouge in the corridor still remains as a reminder of this event.

The trail continues westward into the small town of Poplar Grove. Although there is no designated parking area in this town, parking is available on side streets. The trail heads west out of Poplar Grove, continuing for about two miles to its current western terminus at State Route 76.

Boone County Conservation District currently is seeking funds to develop a continuation of the route that will run through Caledonia and into Roscoe in Winnebago County, where the Stone Bridge Trail begins.

McHenry County Prairie Trail (South)

Endpoints: Algonquin (Kane County Line) to Crystal Lake

Location: McHenry County

Length: 5.5 miles

Surface: Asphalt

Uses:

Contact: Steve Gulgren
McHenry County Conservation District
6512 Harts Road
Ringwood, IL 60072
815-678-4431

◆◆◆

While currently only 5.5 miles, this trail is the southern portion of the 20-mile Prairie Trail that will connect the Wisconsin border to Kane County's 35-mile Fox River Trail by the end of 1994.

Even at its present length, this relatively short trail offers unusual diversity. From the trail, which parallels an active rail line some of its length, you get an interesting glimpse into gravel mining (the county's largest industry), as well as a rare look at some of Illinois' native prairie.

You will find the northern terminus of McHenry County Prairie Trail (South) at Crystal Lake Avenue, about a mile west of Illinois State Route 31. The current trailhead and ample parking are about a mile south of this point. No public lots are located near Crystal Lake Avenue, although several shopping plazas are nearby. Constructed

McHENRY COUNTY PRAIRIE TRAIL (SOUTH)

Terracotta Ave

Crystal Lake Ave

Crystal Lake

CRYSTAL LAKE

Virginia Rd

Pyott Rd

Algonquin-Cary Rd

Randall Rd

Huntly Algonquin Rd

Fox River

ALGONQUIN

McHenry Co.
Kane Co.

N

FOX RIVER
TRAIL

0   .25 .50 .75   1
SCALE (miles)

during the fall of 1993, the first mile (south to Virginia Avenue) parallels an active rail line and lacks landscaping.

After crossing Virginia Avenue, you will pass the trail parking lot, constructed as the trailhead for the trail's first 4.5 miles, which opened in 1990. The trail, still quite flat and straight, quickly takes on a more natural feel, with pockets of rare species of "hill prairie" lining the trail's east side.

In less than a mile, a turn-of-the-century gravel wash plant is located on the west side of the trail, while formerly-mined gravel pits surround the trail. The active gravel mining area starts where the fence begins to parallel the trail. On the west side of the trail you will see a huge conveyor that crosses over the trail—and eventually carries the gravel to an operating wash plant.

A small wetland on the trail's east side offers insight into the pre-mined look of southern McHenry County. Numerous threatened plants, as well as more than 15 species of colorful (and now-endangered) prairie, line the trail. The county plans to dedicate this area as a nature preserve, with a bench and some interpretive signs.

Barbed-wire fence and the reappearance of the huge conveyor signal the start of another active gravel mine—the trail provides an intriguing view of it. The most interesting aspect may be the seemingly endless conveyor, which looks like a colossal Erector Set as it

Crossing the scenic Fox River near Algonquin

heads toward the wash plant. Here, the gravel is washed, processed into stone sizes and dumped into trucks, which create perhaps the world's largest piles of sand.

The face of the trail changes quickly, as the gravel pit ends and a tranquil, 25-acre nature preserve envelopes the trail. A 225-foot bridge over Huntley-Algonquin Road announces that civilization remains nearby. The quaint town of Algonquin has a number of restaurants and shops, some catering to trail users. Just prior to State Route 31, you will pass the Prairie Trail Bike Shop, whose owner plans to develop the building adjacent to the trail into a trail-oriented restaurant.

You are nearing the end of the McHenry County Prairie Trail when you cross the scenic Fox River. The trail's official endpoint is Souwanas Street, although, if you're just getting warmed up, the Fox River Trail (see page 134) continues on the same corridor for 35 miles in Kane County.

North Shore Bike Path

Endpoints: Wisconsin state line to Lake Bluff

Location: Lake County

Length: 14.7 miles

Surface: Crushed limestone

Uses:

Contact: Martin G. Buehler, Director of Transportation
Lake County Division of Transportation
600 W. Winchester Road
Libertyville, IL 60048
708-362-3950

◆◆◆

The North Shore Bike Path "begins" at the Illinois/Wisconsin border, although the Kenosha County Bike Trail continues on the same corridor for almost four miles north to Kenosha, Wisconsin. And, it currently "ends" in Lake Bluff, where the Green Bay Trail travels on the same corridor—next to an active rail line— more than nine miles south to Wilmette (except for a gap in Highwood).

A northern trailhead does not exist for the North Shore Path, which gets it name from the former North Shore Railroad. To reach the Illinois portion of the trail, take State Route 173 east from Interstate 94 and travel approximately five miles to Lewis Avenue. Go north for about 1.5 miles to Russell Road, which is the dividing line of Illinois and Wisconsin. As you head east on Russell, you will see the trail overpass (with a Lake County Bike Route sign) within a half-mile.

NORTH SHORE BIKE PATH

KENOSHA COUNTY
BIKE PATH

SCALE (miles)
0   1   2   3

N

Wisconsin
Illinois
Russell Rd

WINTHROP
HARBOR

Lewis Ave

P

9th St

Sheridan Rd

173

21st St

ZION

29th St

Delany Rd

Wadsworth Rd

ILLINOIS
BEACH
STATE
PARK

Yorkhouse Rd

Green Bay Rd

Golf Rd

WAUKEGAN

Grand Ave

41

Washington St

Belvidere Rd

Lewis Ave

14th St

NORTH CHICAGO

41

Argonne Dr

M.L.King Jr Dr

Buckley Rd

41

Sheridan Rd

Lake
Michigan

176

Rockland Rd

At this location, parking is virtually non-existent and access is attained by scrambling up a moderately steep grade from Russell Road to the trail. (About a mile south, where the trail crosses 9th Street, parking is available.) No specific trail parking lots have been developed along the trail, so use area streets where possible.

If you get on the trail at the border, you can head south toward Chicago's northern suburbs, or you can go north into Wisconsin. If you go north, you will travel about 3.5 miles through primarily residential areas to the intersection of 89th and 30th Streets where the trail ends just south of Kenosha.

If you head south, you will see a sign stating "Begin Lake County North Shore Path" and a 0.0 mile marker. The trail heads due south, with several overpasses to aid travel over busy streets and mile markers to gauge your distance. For the first few miles, you will pass through a number of residential areas, although a swath of green gives the trail a pleasant sense of isolation.

When you reach the Illinois 173 (21st Street) overpass, you may opt to take a side-trip (on-street) to the north unit of the Illinois Beach State Park, home to the only remaining beach ridge shoreline in the state. After crossing over 21st Street, the trail becomes the Zion Bike Path, paralleling Galilee Avenue and becoming asphalt for 1.5 miles. You can take 29th Street about a mile east to Sheridan Avenue, where you will find Zion's quaint downtown area and numerous restaurants.

The reappearance of the crushed stone trail signals that you are once again on the North Shore Bike Path. Soon you will pass mile marker 4, followed by a bridge over Wadsworth Road, which leads to the south entrance of the Illinois Beach State Park. The trail continues south for a couple of miles through primarily residential areas, some of which are still under development.

In the city of Waukegan (the Lake County Seat), telephone lines parallel the route, which begins to take on a light-industrial feel. The trail crosses Washington Street's four lanes at-grade, so use the crosswalk and some caution. A middle school lies along the trail, which many children use during the afternoons.

Soon after Belvidere Street, the trail crosses into North Chicago, where the trail takes on an even more industrial feel, amplified by the surrounding power and telephone lines. As you cross over 14th Street (more than 11 miles into your trip), the trail eases back into a

Touring the North Shore.

residential area and the trail corridor cuts through a boulevard of green. This is enhanced by Neville Park, followed by Boak Park.

At this point, the trail, which has quickly reverted to an industrial setting, goes on-street for several blocks. Take Commonwealth Avenue (under the railroad tracks) for approximately three blocks. Follow bike route signs, which should lead you left (east) onto Martin Luther King Jr. Drive and over the Amstutz Expressway.

The trail then resumes paralleling Sheridan Road (on the sidewalk) near the Great Lakes Naval Training Center. This several-block diversion is scheduled for reconstruction during 1994 to better separate the trail from the busy roads; contact the Lake County Division of Transportation for the current status.

Technically, the North Shore Bike Path ends when the trail resumes along Sheridan Road, however the corridor continues for several miles on the same alignment. You will notice signs first for the Sheridan Trail, followed by Lake Bluff Trail signs when the trail turns to asphalt. This is the beginning of the Green Bay Trail.

Within about 2.5 miles you will reach the beautiful Village of Lake Bluff Train Station, which dates back to 1906. The parking lot requires a permit Monday through Friday (6 a.m. to 6 p.m.) and for overnight stays. However, this lot allows public parking on the weekends, making it a possible starting point. This lot, just a few blocks from charming downtown Lake Bluff, is located at the corner of Sheridan Road and East Scranton Avenue, just north of Illinois State Route 176.

The Illinois Beach State Park

The 6.5-mile shoreline of Illinois Beach State Park has dramatic dunes, sprawling marshes, forests of oak and an incredible array of animal life and vegetation—more than 650 plant species have been recorded in the dunes area. This state park envelops the only remaining beach ridge shoreline in all of Illinois.

If you are exploring the North Shore Bike Path (especially during summer months), allow for a several-hour trip—or even an overnight—to the State Park.

To get to the northern unit of the beach park from the trail, take State Route 173 east for one mile to Sheridan Road, a haven for fast-food restaurants on either end of Zion's quaint downtown. From Sheridan, go a half-mile north to 17th Street, which travels about two miles east to the park's entrance. The actual beach parking area, where you will find restrooms and seasonal concessions, is another mile away.

To get to the park's southern unit from the trail, take Wadsworth Road one mile east from the trail to Sheridan Road, where entrance signs lead you into the park. In addition to a beach, this section of the park offers camping, picnicking and a nature center.

If you still have some energy, you can continue south on the paved Green Bay Trail, which travels more than 10 miles south to Wilmette (except for a gap in Highwood). In addition, Lake County is developing a nine-mile east-west trail on the Mundelein Spur of the North Shore Railroad, which you will cross just south of State Route 176.

River Trail of Illinois

Endpoints: East Peoria to Morton

Location: Tazwell County

Surface: Asphalt

Length: 5.3 miles (will be 9 miles when completed)

Uses:

Contact: Jim Couts, Director
Fon du Lac Park District
201 Veterans Drive
East Peoria, IL 61611
309-699-3923

◆◆◆

The River Trail of Illinois is one of the state's most rapidly growing trails. Since its dedication in May 1991, the trail has run for 5.3 miles between Morton and East Peoria. The Fon du Lac Park District's hard work and recent funding success will go a long way toward making this trail a major component of a trail network in the Peoria area.

Plans call for the River Trail, which is developed on an abandoned interurban Illinois Terminal System line, to eventually connect with the Rock Island Trail to the north and with the City of Pekin to the south. Construction to extend the trail in both directions is scheduled to begin during 1994.

The trail's eastern end currently begins in Bunnel Park, just off Hawthorne street in Morton. Parking and seasonal restroom facilities are available at the park. Once on the trail, you will be heading northwest toward the river. You will cross a few streets as you pass

RIVER TRAIL OF ILLINOIS

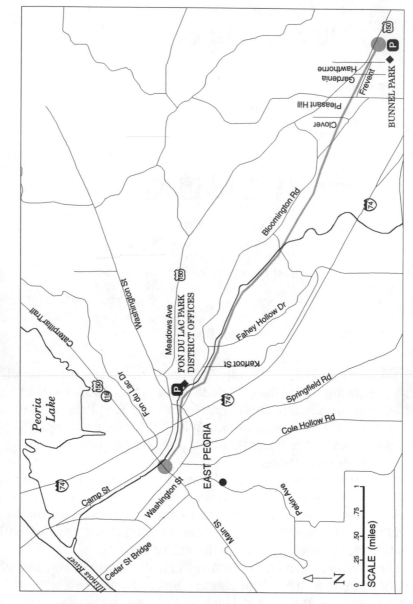

A view of a snowy egret from the trail.

through a quiet residential area, and within a mile you will find yourself in a heavily-wooded area. A variety of birds, trees and wildflowers—including large patches of Beebalm—make this a very pleasant section of the trail from spring to fall.

While in this wooded area, you will begin a leisurely descent down the river bluffs, which for makes for easy cycling and walking when heading toward the river. On the return, however, your muscles may notice the slight incline.

After traveling nearly two miles through the woods, the trail comes to the bottom of the bluff. You are now approaching the commercial area of East Peoria, where you can find several restaurants near the trail as well as the Fon du Lac Park District office (and parking). The trail crosses a few busy roads, so use caution.

The trail continues for another half-mile from the Park District office, under Interstate 74 to its current terminus near Main Street in East Peoria. Eventually, the trail will continue to the Robert Michel Bridge, where it will cross over the Illinois River, go into Peoria and one day connect to the Rock Island Trail (see next page).

Rock Island Trail State Park

Endpoints: Pioneer Parkway to Toulon

Location: Peoria and Stark Counties

Length: 28 miles

Surface: Crushed Limestone

Uses:

Contacts: Paul Oltman, Trail Ranger
Rock Island State Trail Park
P.O. Box 64
Wyoming, IL 61491
309-243-9156

George Burrier
701 East Polk Street
Morton IL 61550
309-266-5085

◆◆◆

The Rock Island Trail may well be one of the most controversial rail-trail conversions of all time. The battle over this abandoned rail corridor lasted for more than 15 years and included arson, shouting matches, threats, and of course, politics.

When the battle finally ended and the dust settled, the Rock Island Trail became the first rail-trail owned and operated by the Illinois Department of Conservation. Now one of the state's most popular trails, virtually everyone agrees that it was worth the fight.

One of the places to access the trail's southern terminus is the parking area just west of Alta. Public facilities are available at the

ROCK ISLAND TRAIL STATE PARK

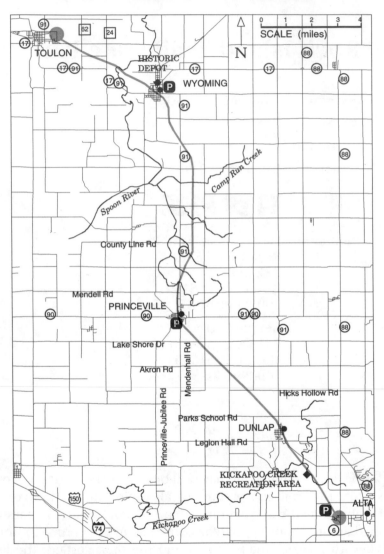

parking area, and a bike shop just down the road can provide any last minute items you may need for the ride.

Once on the trail, you will find yourself traveling through a virtual tunnel of trees with branches arching high overhead. Within about two miles you will come to the Kickapoo Creek Recreation Area. Primitive camping, which is only accessible from the trail, is available at this site as are pit toilets, picnic tables, fire pads and water. Contact the trail ranger to make plans for staying overnight at this site.

In this area you will pass through an intriguing arched culvert, carved from massive limestone blocks. Next, the trail crosses over Kickapoo Creek and then into Dunlap, where the trail moves onto streets and sidewalks.

The Rock Island Trail uses city streets in all of the small towns through which it passes, so watch for trail signs. Also, many of the towns have stores, gas stations and accommodations.

The trail continues from Dunlap, where it passes another parking area at Parks School Road. From here, the trail runs through Illinois farmland as it heads toward Princeville. Once in town, the trail again moves off the abandoned rail corridor, so follow the signs.

Turning north, the trail leaves Princeville on its journey to Wyoming. At the Peoria and Stark County line, you will find a remnant tall grass prairie, which offers you a glimpse of the landscape that greeted area travelers 200 years ago.

As the trail winds into Wyoming, you will pass the Chicago, Burlington and Quincy Railroad Depot, which was built in 1871 and completely restored by the Friends of the Rock Island Trail during

Strolling over the scenic Spoon River

the long battle to build the trail. This "Friends" group successfully got the depot listed on the National Register of Historic Places, then donated it to the state at the trail's grand opening celebration on May 12, 1990. The depot now serves as the Department of Conservation's trail headquarters.

The trail moves onto streets again through Wyoming. After passing through town, the trail crosses the Spoon River on a steel trestle bridge. Once over the river, the trail finishes its final leg and heads toward its northern terminus at a local park in Toulon. Public facilities are available at the parking lot on the trail just south of Toulon, as are restaurants and other amenities in town.

Plans call for linking the Rock Island Trail with the River Trail of Illinois (see page 169) and two-mile Pimiteoui Trail in Peoria. Construction of these linkages should begin by mid-1994, and will lead to a major trail network that runs throughout the Peoria area.

Rock River Recreation Path

Endpoints: Rockford to Loves Park

Location: Winnebago County

Length: 3.3 miles

Surface: Asphalt

Uses:

Contact: Vance Barrie, Marketing Coordinator
Rockford Park District
1401 North Second Street
Rockford, IL 61107-3086
815-987-8694

◆◆◆

Despite its status as one of Illinois' shorter rail-trails, the Rock River Recreation Path is an outstanding 3.3-mile recreation corridor that includes four parks, several sculptures, a rose garden, a boat launch, a trolley and much more—all adjacent to the scenic Rock River. And, on a summer day, you can expect to join half of Rockford's population on the trail!

The trail begins near the YMCA on Y Boulevard, located just north of Rockford on North Second Street (Illinois State Route 251). Y Boulevard ends at a series of parking lots that serve the trail as well as the YMCA's Administration Building, Physical Education Building and Log Lodge. Opened in 1947, this attractive log structure is most often used as a meeting room.

You can easily access the trail from the parking lot, where from May to September, you also can take a ride on the nearby trolley or a short cruise on the 49-passenger Forest City Queen excursion boat.

ROCK RIVER RECREATION PATH

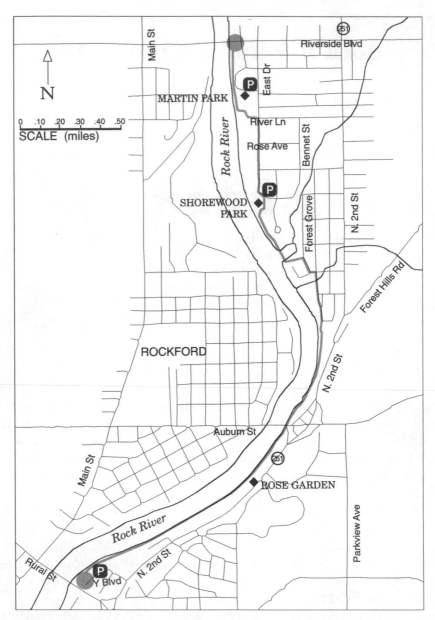

Vance Barrie

A typical early summer day on the Rock River Recreation Path

Or, try your luck at fishing—you will find many suitable fishing spots along the trail's first mile. At this point, the trail hugs the river, which is home to smallmouth bass, largemouth bass, walleye and pike. Follow posted fishing regulation signs.

Markers along the trail at half-mile intervals help you gauge your distance. Just before the half-mile point, you will reach a greenhouse and gardens, which is open year-round. Just beyond the gardens, you will pass a lagoon that houses ducks and swans in the summer and doubles as an ice rink in the winter.

Next, you should take some time to wander through the adjacent Rose Garden, which displays more than 3,000 rose plants. Be sure to catch a glimpse of the 30-foot working floral clock in the garden's center. When the weather is warm, refreshments are available just a short distance away.

Just before you reach the first mile marker, you will pass a 30-ton, 47-foot-high orange sculpture that was moved to its trailside location in 1984. After crossing under the Auburn Street Bridge, you pass through Riverby park, over Spring Creek and past Illinois Street Park before the trail temporarily heads on-street just past the one-and-a-half-mile point.

After mile marker 2, the trail passes a wildlflower prairie area and is again separated from nearby streets as it heads into Shorewood Park. Inside the park, you can explore the Wet Marsh Observation Walk with its abundance of birds, frogs and deer. On Wednesday and Friday evenings from May through August, catch the award-winning Rockford Ski Broncs' entertaining water ski show. Bleachers, concessions and restrooms are available for spectators.

Beyond Shorewood Park, you will be back on-street through a residential area for about five blocks. At River Lane, the trail heads off-street and into Martin Park, which offers a playground, restrooms, concessions, pay phones, a shelter and two memorials. The action-packed trail ends at the Riverside Boulevard Bridge, which provides access to North Towne Mall and several restaurants.

The incredible array of interesting activities make this trail a popular destination, especially for local residents. The Rock River Recreation Path is worth a visit just to see how one community incorporated a rail-trail into a complete recreation network.

Vadalabene Great River Road Bike Trail

Endpoints: .5 miles west of Alton to Pere Marquette State Park

Location: Madison and Jersey Counties

Length: 3.5 miles of 20-mile trail is on an abandoned rail line

Surface: Asphalt

Uses:

Contact: Ron Tedesco
Illinois Department of Transportation
1100 Eastport Plaza Drive
P.O. Box 988
Collinsville, IL 62234-6198
618-346-3100

◆◆◆

During the Great Flood of 1993 the Vadalabene Great River Road Bike Trail was better suited for a canoe than a bicycle. Paralleling the Mississippi River for its entire length, the trail is now back above sea level, but still offering an up-close and personal experience with the legendary Mississippi River.

Named after Sam Vadalabene, a long-time Illinois State Senator and trail proponent, the trail begins at a parking lot a half-mile west of Alton on State Route 100 (the Great River Road). At this point, the trail is a separate path that runs between the Great River Road and the base of the towering bluffs. A short distance past the parking

VADALABENE GREAT RIVER ROAD BIKE TRAIL

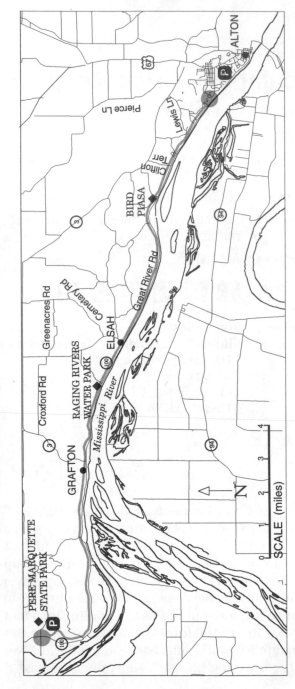

lot, you might see a small waterfall flowing down the bluff and under the trail.

Within about two miles, you will come to a replica of the "Bird Piasa" up on the bluff. Legend has it that explorers Joliet and Marquette saw the original Piasa Bird pictograph painted on the cliffs as they paddled up the river more than 300 years ago. The pictograph represented an underwater jaguar spirit feared by the Native American tribes, who believed that the spirit lurked in the river searching for victims to drown.

As with many legends, the truth often gets distorted over the years. Illinois novelist John Russell may have created the legend in 1836, and an Illinois artist apparently painted the original depiction of the bird.

About three miles west of the Piasa Bird, you will pass a parking lot where the trail enters Jersey County, just off Stanka Lane. At the 6.7-mile point, the trail moves onto the shoulders of the Great River Road. The trail's westbound traffic stays on the north side of the road, with the eastbound traffic on the south side next to the river. A restaurant and the Piasa Boat launch are located here. Some of the bridges on this shared shoulder are narrow, so use caution and watch for traffic as you cross them.

After traveling about 3.5 miles along the shared shoulder, you will come to the historic town of Elsah. Almost 80 percent of the town's existing structures, many of which sit charmingly nestled in the bluffs, were built between 1850 and 1890. Take a detour to explore, browse and eat in Elsah's restaurants, quaint shops and bed and breakfasts.

Back out on the trail, the shared shoulder continues, and almost 3.5 miles from Elsah, you will come to the Raging Rivers Water Park at Palisades Parkway. This park, complete with water slide and swimming pool, offers a great diversion for kids of all ages.

Just past the water park is the town of Grafton, near the confluence of the Illinois and Mississippi Rivers. The town once thrived on the fishing and boating industries, and during the 1850s, it was the largest fresh water fishing port on the Mississippi River. As you enter Grafton, the westbound lane of the trail crosses the highway to join the eastbound lane through the town's side streets.

Prior to the devastating flood of 1993, plans called for the trail to continue through Grafton as a designated trail. However, at the

The Mississippi on one side and scenic bluffs on the other.

time of this writing all plans for the trail's course through town have been delayed while the residents recover from flood damage. When this section is finally complete, it will be adequately marked to guide you through town to the section of trail that continues to Pere Marquette State Park.

Just west of Grafton stands a monument commemorating Marquette and Joliet's 1673 voyage through the area; a parking area near the monument provides another access point to the trail. At this point, the trail again separates from the highway and rolls along through the hills.

As you near Pere Marquette State Park, nearly 20 miles from the starting point, you pass the park's camping area. Go a half-mile further and you will arrive at the northwestern endpoint of the trail in the parking lot of the Pere Marquette Lodge. The park emcompasses more than 8,000 acres and abounds with wildlife. For additional information on the park call 618-786-3323, and for the lodge, call 618-786-2331.

Plans call for the trail to continue into Alton along the highway, travel through town, cross the river on a new bridge and head into Missouri. The ultimate connection, supported by many in the area, will eventually link to Missouri's 200-mile Katy Trail State Park, making the Vadalabene Great River Road Bike Trail a key section of the longest, two-state trail—and an important component of a nationwide trail network.

The Bird Plasa

Fox Valley Park District

Trailing behind on the wooded Virgil L. Gilman Nature Trail

Virgil L. Gilman Nature Trail

Endpoints: Sugar Grove to Aurora

Location: Kane County

Length: 12 miles

Surface: Asphalt and crushed stone

Uses:

(in designated areas)

Contacts: Charles E. Hoscheit, Director
Fox Valley Park District
P.O. Box 818
Aurora, IL 60507
708-897-0516

◆ ◆ ◆

Named after the Fox Valley Park District's first director, the Virgil Gilman Nature Trail is a tribute to his vision for a trail system in the Fox Valley. Built in the late 1950s and designated as a National Heritage Trail during the early 1990s, this trail offers a scenic mix of woods, farmland and marshes blended with a few residential and light-industrial areas.

Bliss Woods Forest Preserve, which is a half-mile east of Illinois State Route 47 on Bliss Road, is the western terminus of the Virgil Gilman Nature Trail. The Forest Preserve—which includes a camping area—offers numerous picnic tables, a shelter, parking and restrooms in a peaceful green setting. The asphalt trail begins at the intersection of Bliss Road and the preserve's second entrance, which is signed as the camping area entrance.

VIRGIL L. GILMAN NATURE TRAIL

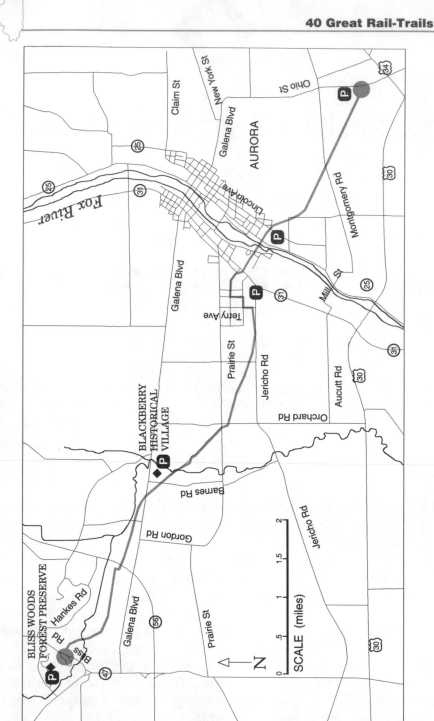

Shrouded in trees for the first couple of miles, the Virgil Gilman Nature Trail is a pleasant respite from the continually-developing areas near Aurora and Chicago's far western suburbs. In less than two miles the trail reaches State Route 56, a four-lane, 55-mile-per-hour road. While an underpass currently exists for trail users, it is often full of water, rendering it useless unless you are in the mood to get a bit wet. At this time, the only alternative is to cross at-grade using an exceptional dose of caution. Fortunately, a median divides the four lanes of traffic, so you can cross two lanes at a time.

At several subsequent road crossings, you will notice one of the trail's intriguing design details: a series of elaborate stone walls that prevent motorized vehicles from accessing the trails. The walls' built-in benches and sun-dials double as pleasant rest stops for trail users.

After crossing Galena Boulevard, the trail approaches the Black-berry Farm Historical Village. This outdoor folk museum with a turn-of-the-century motif, includes a town square, museums, demonstrations, an antique carousel, a short train ride and picnicking facilities. A popular family destination, this seasonal park is open daily from late April to early September and weekends through October. Sharing the same parking lot with the historical village, the George W. Austin Photovoltaic Project is worth a stop if you are interested in energy.

In another mile, the trail crosses Prairie Street and Orchard Road before paralleling an active rail line for about a mile. Still surrounded by trees, the trail runs through an older residential area after separating from the active railroad tracks. At the next parking area, near the intersection of Terry Avenue and Jericho Road, the trail is diverted to a series of streets for several blocks, and the trail's surroundings make an abrupt change to a light-industrial setting.

A "you are here" trail map with directions is posted on the trail just prior to Terry Avenue. To follow the trail route, take a left onto Terry, a right onto Rathbone Avenue, a left onto Elmwood Drive and a right onto Ridgeway Drive. After crossing over a couple of sets of on-street railroad tracks, you come to a small trailhead where the Virgil L. Gilman Nature Trail resumes. You quickly go under Lake Street and two sets of active tracks. In the vicinity you also will find Copley Park, offering restrooms, a playground and a snack shop.

The trail crosses the scenic Fox River on a beautiful steel trestle. On the east side of the Fox River, the Virgil L. Gilman Trail temporarily continues its light-industrial feel, but gives way to a pleasant, wooded residential area and a series of community parks after crossing over Lincoln Avenue.

For the last mile, the trail continues southeast and eases into a surprisingly rural setting. Near the Kane/Kendall County line, the Virgil L. Gilman Trail makes a rather anti-climactic ending at U.S. Route 30. A small trailhead with a few parking spaces marks the trail's end.

Fox Valley Park District

One of the many intricate stone structures designed to prevent motorized access while doubling as rest stops.

An Introduction to Rail-Trails in Indiana

While Indiana has only six existing rail-trails, more than 25 projects are underway throughout the state. A number of these rail-trail efforts are centered in the northwest portion of Indiana, where they can link into developing trail networks in Illinois and Michigan.

As with most Midwestern states, Indiana had an extensive network of railroad corridors. In the late 1800s, the state's railroad mileage peaked at nearly 7,500 miles; by the early 1990s, almost half of the railroad system had been abandoned. To preserve these rail corridors, neighborhood associations, local businesses and trail user groups formed the Hoosier Rails-to-Trails Council in 1987 to save the Monon Corridor near Indianapolis and eventually to promote rail-trails throughout the state.

Although local opposition has stalled a number of Indiana rail-trail projects, the future is looking brighter in the Hoosier State. In 1993, a Muncie-based, public-private partnership secured a 51-mile rail corridor in the east-central part of the state, which will be converted into the Cardinal Greenway and will become the state's longest rail-trail. During the same year, Monroe County received funding for the 15-mile Limestone Country Trail near Bloomington.

The three Indiana trails highlighted in this book are excellent examples of the variety Indiana has to offer. From endangered prairie plants, to limestone bluffs to riverfront vistas, the rail-trails of Indiana are well worth a visit!

INDIANA'S GREAT RAIL-TRAILS

1. East Bank Trail
2. Limestone Country Trail
3. Prairie-Duneland Trail

East Bank Trail

Endpoints: South Bend

Location: St. Joseph County

Length: 5.25 miles of a 7.5-mile trail is on an abandoned rail corridor

Surface: Asphalt

Uses:

Contact: Karl Stevens
South Bend Parks Department
301 South St. Louis Boulevard
South Bend, IN 46617
219-235-9401

◆ ◆ ◆

The East Bank Trail is the Indiana portion of the Blossomland River Trail, which will extend 35 miles from South Bend, Indiana to Lake Michigan at St. Joseph-Benton Harbor, Michigan.

Beginning at the campus of Indiana University South Bend, the trail follows along the east bank of the beautiful St. Joseph River. While this is an urban area serving more than a quarter of a million people, the trail is in a relatively natural area of interconnected riverfront parks.

After passing the popular Farmer's Market, the trail does not have a surface street crossing for the next two miles. In the downtown area, the trail parallels the East Race Waterway. This reconstructed millrace canal is one of only four built kayak courses in the world. Olympic canoe and kayaking events are held in addition to innertubing for the general public.

EAST BANK TRAIL

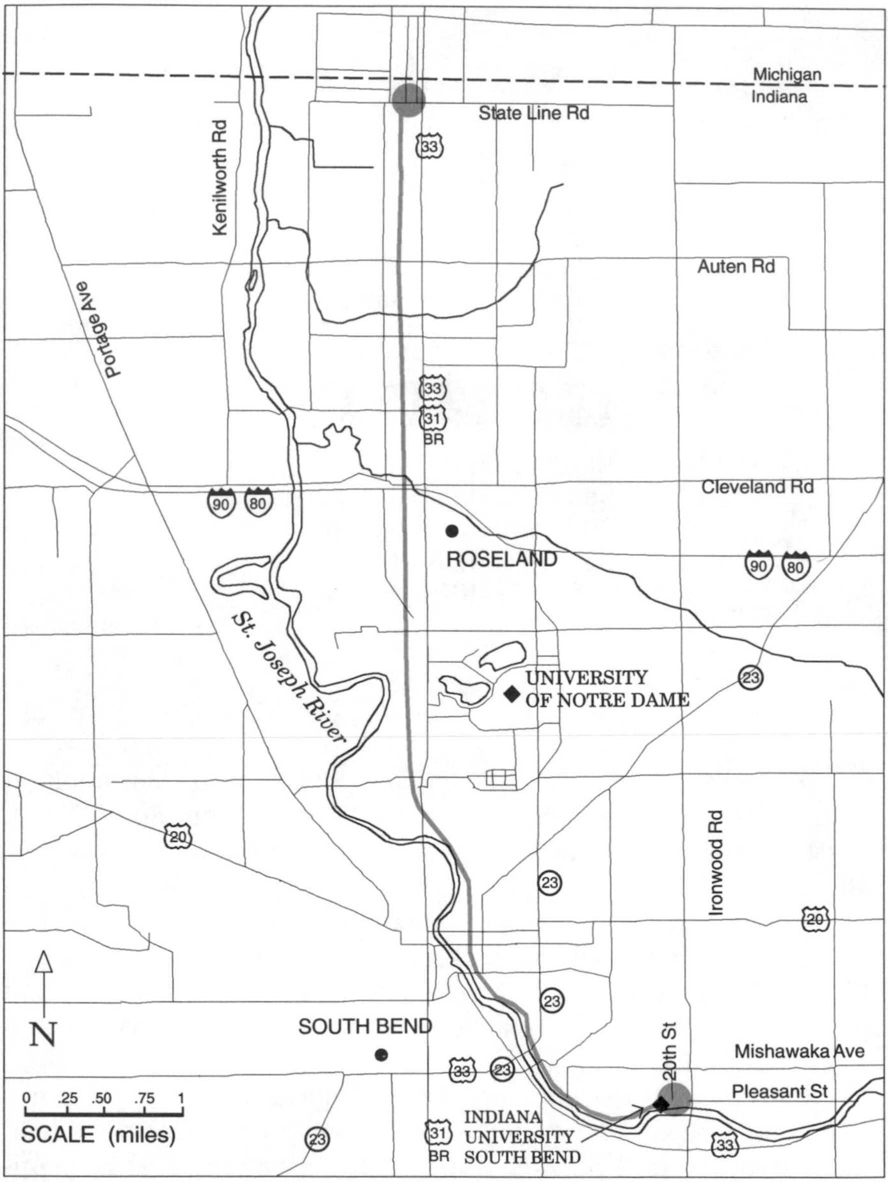

Michigan
Indiana

State Line Rd

33

Kenilworth Rd

Portage Ave

Auten Rd

33
31
BR

90 80

Cleveland Rd

St. Joseph River

ROSELAND

90 80

UNIVERSITY
OF NOTRE DAME

23

20

Ironwood Rd

23

20

N

23

SOUTH BEND

20th St

Mishawaka Ave

Pleasant St

0   .25 .50 .75   1

33 23

SCALE (miles)

33

23

31 INDIANA
BR UNIVERSITY
    SOUTH BEND

33

Paralleling the St. Joseph River

Leaving the historic East Bank, the trail climbs out of the valley to the University of Notre Dame area. The majority of South Bend's 20,000 college students live in this neighborhood. The trail first traverses the campus of Holy Cross College on its way to St. Marys College.

At the entry drive to St. Mary's College, you can cross the busy street at the stoplight and enter the 2,000-acre University of Notre Dame. A system of trails interconnect forests, gardens, two lakes and more than 100 architecturally-significant buildings. Known locally as the "Emerald Isle," this campus offers one of the most pleasing environments anywhere.

Back on the main trail, you continue north toward Michigan. Scheduled for completion in mid-1994, this 4.5-mile section enters a suburban area. You will see residential areas on the west of the trail, and on the east you will see commercial development, including several motels.

North of busy Cleveland Road (Business U.S. 31) the trail crosses over Juday Creek, which is the only brown trout spawning stream in Indiana. The sunken gardens to the east are the remnants of a large estate, now the grounds of a motor lodge. Kiefer Creek is the last water crossing before entering Michigan.

Construction is scheduled to begin on the Michigan portion of the Blossomland River Trail in 1994. This 35-mile trail will connect the towns of Niles and Berrien Springs to Lake Michigan through the orchards and vineyards of Berrien County.

Limestone Country Trail

Endpoints: Bloomington to Lawrence County Line

Location: Monroe County

Length: 15 miles (scheduled for completion by the end of 1994)

Surface: Currently original ballast; will be asphalt when completed

Uses:

(when surface is complete)

Contact: Monroe County Parks and Recreation
119 West 7th Street
Bloomington, IN 47404
812-333-3800

◆ ◆ ◆

Although the Limestone Country Trail is not officially open at this writing, the spectacular countryside through which it passes merits its inclusion. Monroe County Parks and Recreation expects to open the trail to hiking on June 4, 1994, National Trails Day.

Presently, the trail's surface consists of the heavy ballast left behind by the railroad salvage crews during 1993. While this surface is adequate for hiking, it makes for a very rough ride, even on a mountain bike. Plans call for paving the surface by late fall of 1994.

Built in 1847, this line made the Indiana limestone industry possible. The New Albany Salem Railroad, one of the state's first railroads, connected the Ohio River to Lake Michigan and provided

LIMESTONE COUNTRY TRAIL

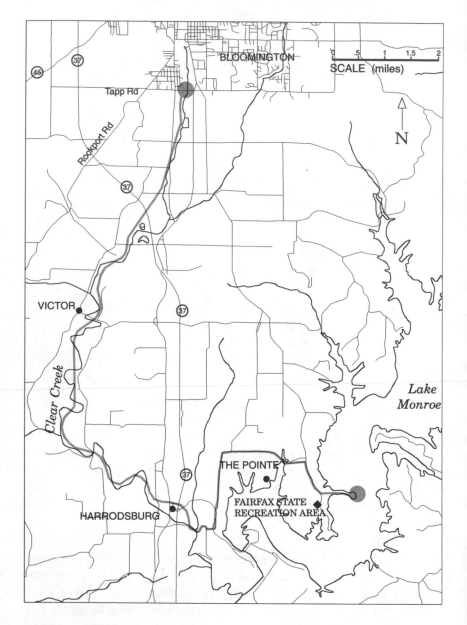

numerous markets for the valuable stone. The corridor also was operated by the Monon Railroad, as well as CSX, before it filed for abandonment early in 1993.

The trail begins its winding run through limestone country at Tapp Road on the southwest side of Bloomington (home to the beautiful campus of Indiana University). Here, the trail passes through a quiet residential and light-industrial area. After nearly two miles, the trail moves beyond the residential and light-industrial areas and heads into a very hilly, rural setting.

For much of its length, the trail maintains a close relationship with Clear Creek, emphasized by the 15 bridges over the creek in the same number of miles. The creek crossings provide numerous opportunities for visitors to enjoy the beauty of the water-carved limestone bluffs. Beaver activity also is noticeable, and ducks can be seen in some of the pools. The variety and volume of wildlife are among the trail's best features.

Between the creek crossings, the trail passes through scenic pasture land, picturesque fields and beautiful wooded areas.

In many areas, the trail runs through narrow limestone cuts made before the Civil War. These cuts add appeal to the trail in winter as

Hiking along the undeveloped Limestone Country Trail corridor

water seeping from the rock freezes and forms small natural ice sculptures.

The trail comes to an end short of the Fairfax State Recreation Area, but the county is working on plans that will lead trail users to the beach of Lake Monroe.

Since development of the trail is contingent on the fundraising efforts of the local trail group, contact Monroe County Parks and Recreation for up-to-date information before visiting the trail.

Prairie-Duneland Trail

Endpoints: State Road 149 to the Lake/Porter County line in the City of Portage

Location: Porter County

Length: 2 miles (will be 6 miles when completed)

Surface: Asphalt and original ballast

Uses:

Contact: Carl Fisher, Superintendent
Portage Parks and Recreation Department
2100 Willowcreek Road
Portage, IN 46368
219-762-1675

◆◆◆

Despite its length, the Prairie Duneland Trail offers many historical and natural features. The trail serves as an important host to more than 180 native prairie and wetland plant species including many that are endangered in Indiana. In addition, the trail parallels the route of the Calumet Beach Trail, used by natives in pre-settlement times for travel along the beach areas of Lake Michigan—which was much larger at that time. In fact, archeological sites have been found along the trail corridor.

The central portion of a 21-mile abandonment by the Elgin, Joliet and Eastern Railway in the late 1980s, the trail currently has two paved miles, with a third scheduled to open in 1994. Original railroad ballast remains on the other three miles, which are hikeable and mountain-bikable.

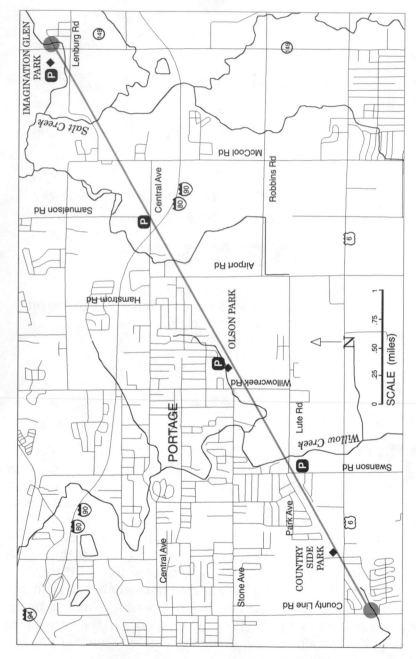

PRAIRIE-DUNELAND TRAIL

The "J," as the railroad line was sometimes called, was constructed in 1888 to serve primarily as a freight line designed to bypass the congested rails near Chicago. The Elgin, Joliet and Eastern Railway Company did experiment with daily first-class runs to the town of Porter, but these passenger trains disappeared in 1907. Interestingly, the company did continue passenger service until the 1960s via a "mixed-train," which primarily consisted of the passengers riding in the caboose.

You can access the paved portion of the Prairie-Duneland Trail near the intersection of Samuelson Road and Central Avenue, where a small gravel parking triangle is located. Portage City Hall and several shops are located about a mile to the west on Central Avenue.

The paved portion of the trail ends about a quarter-mile east of the parking triangle. You may want to travel this short distance east to see the spot where a 5,000-year-old plummet and several projectile points were found along the south edge of the trail corridor. These were from a habitation site dating back to the Archaic and Prehistoric Periods. An unpaved section of the trail continues east for nearly two miles to State Route 149.

Heading west from Samuelson and Central, you will pass under the Interstate 80 Toll Road, followed by a quiet wooded section of trail. While you will see some homes, the trail generally is set apart from any developments.

After crossing a small culvert and stream, the adjacent homes become more numerous and some examples of basic prairie grasses and sedges can be seen along the trail's northern side. Immediately after crossing Airport Road, you can see a small patch of prairie species to the south. The power substation on the north is located along the right-of-way of an old electric interurban line. This defunct line connected Valparaiso and the still-operating South Shore Electric interurban.

After several more residences, you will reach a pine forest on the trail's southern side. The corridor's edge along this private pine forest has several wet prairie and other wetland species. Behind the pines is a shallow pond that attracts a wide variety of waterfowl.

Between the pond and the eastern edge of Olson Park, just north of the trail corridor along the old Willowcreek streambed is another archaeological site. Several artifacts—including a large corner-notched projectile point, several scrapers, and a few small chert

Portage Parks and Recreation Department

A newly-paved portion of the Prairie Duneland Trail

knives—were found in what appeared to be a habitation site dating back to the Prehistoric Period.

Along the southern boundary of Olson Park, you will see a few remaining farm fields mixed with residential homes. After leaving Olson Park, the north side of the corridor remains relatively natural until reaching Willowcreek Road. Several shops, stores and restaurants are less than a mile south at the bustling intersection of Willowcreek Road and U.S. Highway 6.

West of Willowcreek, you enter the section planned for paving in 1994. The trail continues between homes on the north and the YMCA on the south. Just west of the YMCA, is a small wetland area on the trail's south side. This three-acre site, bordered by a small stream, has been donated to the Portage Parks Department and includes several native prairie species.

The area west of the new housing developments stays fairly remote until you near the intersection of Lute and Swanson Roads. Along this section, you will find many native plants. Also, to the north you can see a large historic farm homestead, secluded on its own acreage amidst the newer homes. Woodlands on the north provide a pleasant sense of remoteness.

You will see the trail's western parking triangle as you approach Lute and Swanson Roads. This is the western boundary of the section to be paved in 1994.

The trail continues west to Countryside Park at U.S. Highway 6—pedestrians and adventuresome bicyclists can use this mile-long portion. The Portage Parks Department does own an additional half-mile of corridor south of the highway to the Porter/Lake County Line. This section will be developed when the Lake County Parks Department completes its plans to purchase and develop the 11 remaining miles from the original abandonment.

The Prairie-Duneland Trail is an important link in a Northwestern Indiana trails network. When Lake County completes its portion, the trail will almost reach the eastern border of Illinois. And, when the Town of Chesterton continues trail development on the easternmost four miles of the original abandonment, the trail will extend to within 15 miles of the Michigan border.

Saturn Retailer Locations

Michigan

Saturn North
8400 Dixie Highway
Clarkston, MI 48348
313-620-8800

Saturn of Ann Arbor
500 Auto Mall Drive
Ann Arbor, MI 48103
313-769-3991

Saturn of Farmington Hills
24730 Haggerty Road
Farmington Hills, MI 48335
313-473-7220

Saturn of Grand Rapids
2720 28th Street S.E.
Grand Rapids, MI 49512
616-949-0555

Saturn of Okemos
1728 Grand River Avenue
Okemos, MI 48864
517-347-7890

Saturn of Plymouth
9301 Massey Drive
Plymouth, MI 48170
313-453-7890

Saturn of Saginaw
5330 Bay Road
Saginaw, MI 48604
517-797-8800

Saturn of Southfield
29929 Telegraph Road
Southfield, MI 48034
313-354-6001

Saturn of Southgate
16600 Fort Street
Southgate, MI 48195
313-246-3300

Saturn of Traverse City
1621 South Garfield
Traverse City, MI 49684
616-935-1616

Saturn of Troy
1804 Maplelawn
Troy, MI 48084
313-643-4350

Saturn of Warren
7830 Convention Boulevard
Warren, MI 48093
313-979-2000

Illinois

Saturn of Champaign
1110 Bloomington Road
Champaign, IL 61821
217-352-4700

Saturn of Countryside
6070 LaGrange Road
La Grange, IL 60525
708-352-7832

Saturn of Elgin
1320 East Chicago Road
Elgin, IL 60120
708-882-1800

Saturn of Glenview
630 Waukegan Road
Glenview, IL 60025
708-998-6998

Saturn of Libertyville
1160 South Milwaukee Avenue
Libertyville, IL 60048
708-362-6600

Saturn of Naperville
1661 Aurora Avenue
Naperville, IL 60540
708-717-8118

Saturn of Peoria
2300 West Pioneer Parkway
Peoria, IL 61615
309-691-2500

Saturn of Rockford
343 N. Perryville Road
Rockford, IL 61108
815-394-5400

Saturn of Schaumberg
125 West Higgins Road
Hoffman Estates, IL 60194
708-843-7600

Saturn of South Holland
800 East 162nd Street
South Holland, IL 60473
708-331-6400

Saturn of Springfield
1829 Stevenson Drive
Springfield, IL 62703
217-585-0060

Saturn of Tinley Park
8355 West 159th Street
Tinley Park, IL 60477
708-614-7400

Saturn of Waukegan
500 South Green Bay Road
Waukegan, IL 60085
708-360-5000

Indiana

Saturn of Evansville
5230 Division Street
Evansville, IN 47715
812-471-0011

Saturn of Fort Wayne
910 Avenue of Autos
Fort Wayne, IN 46804
219-436-2252

Saturn of Greenwood
1287 U.S. 31 South
Greenwood, IN 46143
317-865-1551

Saturn of Indianapolis
5333 Pike Plaza
Indianapolis, IN 46254
317-293-1551

Saturn of LaFayette
801 Sagamore Parkway South
Lafayette, IN 47905
317-448-1000

Saturn of Michiana
4028 North Grape Road
Mishawaka, IN 46545
219-258-6333

How to Become a Rails-to-Trails Conservancy Member

RAILS - to - TRAILS
CONSERVANCY

Rails-to-Trails Conservancy is a private, non-profit public charity, supported by the generous contributions of its members and friends —individuals and families like you. We invite you to join today.

Membership/Gift Membership Levels

Individual Membership **$18**

Supporting Membership **$25**

Patron Membership **$50**

Benefactor Membership **$100**

Advocate Membership **$500**

Trailblazer Society Membership **$1,000**

As a member of Rails-to-Trails Conservancy, you will receive the following benefits:

◆ A free subscription to our quarterly newsletter **Trailblazer.**

◆ A free copy of the **Sampler of America's Rail-Trails**.

◆ Discounts on Conservancy publications, merchandise and conferences.

◆ Additional membership benefits for Trailblazer Society members.

And, most importantly, you will get the satisfaction that comes from helping build a nationwide network of beautiful trails for all of us to enjoy for years (and generations) to come.

Why don't you become an RTC member today?
(Use the order form on page 213)

Rails-to-Trails Conservancy Merchandise and Publications

RAILS
- to -
TRAILS
CONSERVANCY

500 Great Rail-Trails

Our most popular publication! This directory offers information such as location, end-points, length, surface material, contacts and allowable uses for 500 rail-trails in 44 states. **500 Great Rail-Trails #GRT** $9.95 (Members $7.95)

RTC short-sleeve T-Shirt

Printed on 100% cotton, this six-panel T-shirt tells the Rails-to-Trails story in an eye-catching turquoise/purple/yellow/black design. Made in U.S.A.; please indicate size on the order form: Small (S), Medium (M), Large (L), X-Large (XL) **#TSS** $16.95 (Members $12.95)

RTC Water Bottle

Quench your thirst with this six-panel design water bottle! This colorful, heavy-duty water bottle holds 28 ounces and the exciting colors match the RTC t-shirt. **#WBBN** $4.95 (Members $3.95)

Secrets of Successful Rail-Trails

If you want to help convert an abandoned corridor into a rail-trail, this book is for you. It offers a step-by-step process for organizing supporters, working with government agencies, getting publicity, finding funds to build a trail and much more! **#SST** $19.95 (Members $16.95)

RTC Sweatshirt

The new RTC crewneck sweatshirt is generously-sized for easy movement. It comes in ash grey with RTC's six-panel design on the front; 80% cotton/20% polyester. **#SWSA** $26.95 (Members $22.95)

Organizing Citizen Support

This 123-page report discusses the five stages of rail-trail development and offers four instructive case histories. **#OCS** $22.95 (Members $18.95)

ORDER FORM

Item Description	Item #	Size	Qty.	Unit Price	Total Amt.
Membership					
Sub-total					
FL, IL, OH, MI, PA & WA Sales Tax					
Shipping & Handling Charge (merchandise & publications ONLY)					
TOTAL					

POSTAGE & HANDLING CHARGES:
If your merchandise total is: Please add:

Up to $15	$4.50
$15.01–$25.00	$5.50
$25.01–$50.00	$6.50
$50.01–$75.00	$7.00
$75.01 and higher	$8.00

ORDERED BY:
Name
Address
City
State & Zip
Phone Number

Please check payment method:
❑ My check, payable to Rails-to-Trails Conservancy, is enclosed.
❑ Please charge my: ❑ MasterCard ❑ VISA
Card # _____ Exp. Date _____
Signature _____

Please return this form (and any payment) to: Rails-to-Trails Conservancy, Shipping Department, P.O. Box 295, Federalsburg, MD 21632-0295. Or, to order by MasterCard or VISA, use our toll-free number: 1-800-888-7747, ext. 11.

Satisfaction guaranteed!

We will ship your order within 10 days of receipt; some items may be sent separately.

Rails-to-Trails Conservancy is a non-profit charitable organization as qualified under Section 501(c)(3) of the Internal Revenue Code. Contributions are tax deductible to the extent permitted by law.

To obtain a copy of the current financial statement, annual report and state registration filed by RTC, contact RTC at 1400 Sixteenth Street, NW, Suite 300, Washington, DC 20036, 202-797-5400.

40GRT

Let Rails-to-Trails Conservancy
know where you would like to see future
Great Rail-Trail guidebooks.

❑ I would like to see a **regional** rail-trail guidebook covering the following states:

_____

_____

_____

❑ I would like to see a **state-specific** rail-trail guidebook for the following state(s):

_____

_____

_____

❑ I would like to receive updates on *40 Great Rail-Trails in Michigan, Illinois and Indiana* and information on future Rails-to-Trails Conservancy guidebooks:

_____

_____

_____

Name_____

Street Address _____

_____

City, State & Zip_____

Return to: Publications Department, Rails-to-Trails Conservancy, 1400 16th Street, NW, Suite 300, Washington, DC 20036.